OUR IOWA

Picture-Perfect Views of Its Beauty and Bounty

Book's Like an Iowa Vacation

"GOSH—I didn't realize Iowa was so *pretty*!"

We hear that comment after every issue of *Our Iowa* magazine—as readers ooh and aah over the vivid photos of our beautiful land.

Sometimes it comes from out-of-state subscribers—former Iowans who've moved away, but subscribe to the magazine to "keep in touch" with their home state.

But we hear it from readers who live in Iowa as well. They may have never traveled to northeast Iowa and wandered the steep limestone bluffs and narrow valleys called "Little Switzerland".

Or they may have never driven the length of the Loess Hills—that narrow band of windblown dunes of soil that rise up out of the Missouri River Valley in western Iowa. There are only two places in the world where these ancient geological formations exist—in China and Iowa.

Other readers are surprised to learn that we still have quaint and idyllic areas like Van Buren County in southeast Iowa, where many Amish live.

Did you know there's not a stoplight or fast-food restaurant in that entire county? Just small farms amid the rolling hills and quaint little villages nestled along the banks of the meandering Des Moines River.

So it's little wonder that readers keep remarking about Iowa's *beauty*.

Finally, we'd heard those comments so often we decided to showcase that beauty in this high-quality coffee-table book. So get a fresh cup of coffee—you're about to take a trip across our state and enjoy the *spectacular scenery* between our borders.

Book 5 Years in the Making

Indirectly we've been working on this book for nearly 5 years. That's when we began publishing *Our Iowa*—the magazine.

In each issue, we include a photo feature called "Io-Ways... Photos Along Our Beautiful Byways and Backroads". We work with some of Iowa's top professional photographers who scour the countryside from river to river—the Missouri and Mississippi—and from Lamoni to Spirit Lake to capture the beauty that is pure "Iowa".

For this book, we've gathered the very best of these photos from past issues and included them in four Io-Ways features—one for each season—leading off with autumn because it's such a glorious time of the year here.

Nothing symbolizes our state like proudly primped and painted farmsteads. With their well-maintained barns, granaries and farmhouses, they're Iowa icons, and we feature one of "The Prettiest Farms in Iowa" in each issue of the magazine.

So we went back over the years and selected the best of the best (whew—what a job that was to decide) for this book. You'll also meet the farm families who live there—they deserve recognition and a pat on the back for all of the hard work that goes into these showplaces.

Giddyap for a Buggy Ride

This book will also take you on an Amish buggy ride...at least you'll feel that way as you read the diary of Amish farm wife Ruby Kuhns on page 46.

In each issue of *Our Iowa*, Ruby keeps a weeklong journal

TO MAP OUT each issue, Roy Reiman and Jerry Wiebel study stacks of letters from subscribers—and say the best ideas come from readers

of life on a farm where she lives with her husband, Jacob, and their 11 children. It's a fascinating glimpse into the Amish community, and we selected one for inclusion in the book.

"Wild turkeys skittered across the road in front of the buggy" writes Ruby in her Sunday journal entry. "Our horse 'Rita' was a little skittish at first, but then trotted calmly on."

There's so much to see and do in Iowa that Bob and Shirley Meyer of Denison spent 10 days touring Iowa north of Highway 30—and didn't see it all! Read about their "all-Iowa vacation" on page 68.

"Heck, we never even got out of northeast Iowa, there was so much to see and do," says Bob, noting that they might someday do a repeat, only south of Highway 30.

This coffee-table book is the next best thing to a vacation like the Meyers took. It lets you tour the Hawkeye State from the comfort of your favorite chair. Vicariously, we'll take you down scenic roads you likely never knew existed.

We'll admit it—putting this book together was far from "work". It was sheer joy as we pored over the hundreds of photos we'd published in *Our Iowa* magazine the past 5 years. Time and again, we said to ourselves, "Readers are right—*we do live in a pretty state!*"

It made us proud to be Iowans.

As you page through it, you'll surely feel the same sense of pride in our state...and proudly display this "celebration of Iowa" on your coffee table for all of your friends and family to see.

Side Note: "*Success is nothing more than doing what you can do well, and doing well whatever you do, without a thought of fame.*" —*Henry W. Longfellow*

The Old Farmer Sez...

"There are no strangers in Iowa. They are just friends you haven't met yet."

OUR IOWA

Picture-Perfect Views of Its Beauty and Bounty

ditor Jerry Wiebel
ublisher Roy Reiman
lanaging Editor Larry Wiebel
rt Director Mary Sailer
opy Editor Kristine Krueger
ditorial Assistant Paula Wiebel
rculation Coordinator Mary Reilly
ookkeeper Suzanne Thompson
ffice Assistants Nancy Wiebel, Jennie Van Voorhis

ublished by *Our Iowa* magazine, 606 Golden Aspen Drive, Suite 109, mes IA 50010. Phone: **1-515/232-0075.** r contact us by E-mail at *editors@OurIowa lagazine.com*. Web site: *www.OurIowa lagazine.com*. ISBN: 978-0-9835596-9-6

ont Cover: Washington County farm, photo by Joseph Stanski
ack Cover: Nashville warbler, photo by Hugh Perry; Hogback Covered Bridge, photo by Gerald Rowles

'ssst! Something's Iidden in This Book!

UBSCRIBERS to *Our Iowa* magazine now we like to add a little fun to each ssue by hiding something within the ages, then award prizes to the finders. It's too involved to explain here; ask subscriber if you aren't one already.)

So, we decided to add that same in-igue to this book. *Somewhere* in these ages we've hidden—fittingly—a tiny rawing of a *wild rose*, our state flower.

If you find it, send a postcard or note aming the page where you spotted hat elusive flower to: *Our Iowa*, 1606 Golden Aspen Drive, Suite 109, Ames A 50010. Deadline: March 29, 2013.

If you've identified the correct page, ve'll then put your entry along with oth-rs into our cracker barrel for the prize rawing. Only one entry per person.

What's the Prize? It's a tasty one! The winner will receive $100.00 worth of coupons that can be used at any of the mall diners listed in our *Directory of owa's Best Ma & Pa Restaurants*. The atest edition is offered on page 87.

If this sounds like fun and the prize ppetizing, enter our bloomin' contest y searching for that hidden wild rose.

FOR ADDITIONAL COPIES of this book, call **1-515/232-0075** and have your credit card handy. Or send mail orders to: *Our Iowa*, 1606 Golden Aspen Drive, Suite 109, Ames IA 50010. Price per book: $18.98 plus $3.95 for shipping.

IO-WAYS

Featuring "awesome autumn" along our byways and backroads.

One wordsmith describes autumn in Iowa as a second spring—when every leaf is a flower. It's an explosion of color from the Missouri River to the Mississippi.

It's also football season, which calls to mind this note from a oteworthy Iowan, 1939 Heisman Trophy winner Nile Kinnick. Ie wrote:

"The changing seasons of the Midwest—the intense heat in ummer, bitter cold in winter, and the unsurpassable beauty and nvigorating weather of fall and spring—is what makes it an nteresting place to live. Only robust and virile people can live n such a climate and enjoy it."

Autumn is our reward for enduring the steamy "dog days" of summer...and its mellow, sunny afternoons are like embers from those fiery days to gently warm us during the winter months that lie ahead.

So come along and join us as some of the best photographers in Iowa take us for a photo tour along the backroads during this special time of year.

NOT-SO-SCARY SCARECROW has reason to smile—what with the spectacular fall colors at this pond in Polk County (far left).

Ty Smedes

PASSING THE BUCK? Our photographer couldn't pass up snapping a shot of this fella in the Des Moines River Valley in central Iowa! Iowa has a reputation for producing some of the country's best trophy bucks.

RIGHT GOLDEN HAZE ON THE MEADOW. The songwriter must've had this farm in Buchanan County in mind. Oh, what a beautiful morning!

LOOKS LIKE AN ALFRED HITCHCOCK MOVIE. Nope, it's not a scene from *The Birds*—just a huge flock of cowbirds in a feeding frenzy as they prepare for fall migration to warmer climes.

Gerald Rowles

THE APPLE OF OUR EYE is crisp, ripe and juicy—jus waiting to be picked in an orchard in Ida County

Vicki McLead

NATURE'S WATERCOLORS. Autumn's heavenly hues are reflected in the waters of a spring-fed lake at Springbrook State Park in Guthrie County

Joseph Stanski

IFE IN THE NOT-SO-FAST LANE. "I snapped this photo in Kalona's Amish country on an ndian summer day with a soft autumn haze in the air," says photographer Joe Stanski of airfield. "It was one of those afternoons when you want to slow down and just say, 'Ahh!'"

Gerald Rowles

IORSE THIEF CAVE at Scenic View Ranch near Monona is aptly named. A horse statue vas stolen from the ranch entrance, only to be found years later. It now guards the cave.

Gerald Rowles

.OTSA LUMBER. Some newly harvested hardwood logs along a quiet timber road in northeast Iowa await a trip to the sawmill. Looks like a fine set of kitchen cabinets in the making!

DROP ANCHOR and you might think you're along the New England seacoast. But this idyllic harbor is actually along the Mississippi River in the town of Clayton—another indication of Iowa's scenic diversity.

Don Poggensee

CLIPPITY-CLOP, CLIPPITY-CLOP of horse hooves once echoed in covered bridges, like the Cedar Bridge in Madison County. Some called 'em "kissing bridges" because many a fella stopped his buggy and stole a kiss from his best girl in the dark of the bridge.

Ty Smedes

EVERYTHING'S DUCKY. Reflecting the autumn hues of the surrounding foliage, the waters of a wetland in Dallas County provide a colorful repose for an equally colorful wood duck.

COUNTING THEIR BLESSINGS. Surrounded by agricultural bounty, it's not hard to do at Soldier Lutheran Church near Soldier in Monona County. There's much to be thankful for.

Stanley Burman

GETTING AN EARFUL—of golden ripe Iowa corn, that is. Did you know that there is always an even number of rows of kernels on an ear of field corn?

WHEW—WHAT A VIEW! You're looking at the Mississippi from Pikes Peak State Park at McGregor. The area was explored by Zebulon Pike, who discovered Colorado's Pikes Peak. (Ours is prettier!)

Julie Habel

CANINE CAPERS. Our photographer spotted a couple of youngsters playing with the pooch at Backbone State Park in Delaware County. Backbone is Iowa's oldest state par

Ty Sme

WILD GOOSE CHASE. As the ɪn was setting over central Iowa, ɐese were on the fly before the ɪow flies. See ya next spring!

OWNRIGHT HEAVENLY is the ɪwn of Elkader in the fall. The ɪayton County community is ɪnked as one of the 10 prettiest ɪwns in Iowa—and we can see ɪhy. That's St. Joseph's Catholic ɪurch amid the glorious color.

Gerald Rowles

Don Poggensee

GONNA BE A GREAT DAY. The sun burns off the last of the morning fog, revealing a spectacle of colors at Moorehead Lake in Ida County. A good day to play hooky and soak it in.

Joseph Stanski

Gerald Rowles

IN THE ROUND. With a silo in the center for feeding, round barns saved steps doing chores compared to rectangles. Another plus: You couldn't get cornered by feed salesmen!

Stanley Buman

OULDN'T PICKET A PRETTIER PLACE for a photo. notographer Joe Stanski didn't have to travel far to ke it—it's in his picket-fenced backyard in Fairfield. here are lots of leaves to rake—but it's worth it, says Joe.

EAVES YOU YEARNING FOR MORE. As a solitary leaf oats downstream (left) and the sun sets on another growg season, we're wistful over the passing of autumn in Iowa.

URN THE PAGE to see a canoeist paddling across tternut Lake in the Shimek State Forest in far southeast wa. They say a good photo is one that "makes you want be there". We sure want to be in the boat with this guy!

HAT CONCLUDES our photo tour of autumn in Iowa. ood thing Iowa has four seasons! See the "Io-Ways" ctions on pages 28, 54 and 74 for more of its beauty.

Tom Cooper; next page: Joseph Stanski

IA 9214 AF
OSCODA

The Prettiest Farm in Iowa

A PLACE TO HORSE AROUND. Traci and Bill Jennings say their farm is a kids' paradise. In the saddle are Jake, 4, Abby, 9, and Elli, 10. Above: The late-afternoon sun casts a warm glow on their farmhouse.

Photos: Gerald Rowles

Nothing symbolizes our state like proudly primped and painted farmsteads. We showcase one of the prettiest in each issue.

THE MINUTE Bill and Traci Jennings spotted the farm we'r featuring as this issue's "Prettiest Farm" near Story City bac in 2002, they heard it whisper, "Buy me."

Story City

Not that it was a showplace back the The 1890 barn, though straight as a strin badly needed siding, and the house was "teardown". Since it hadn't been lived i for years, the yard was overgrown.

What caught their eye was the hilly topography. That's unde standable when you learn that Bill is a farm kid from the Loes Hills of western Iowa, and Traci grew up in the rolling dair country of northeast Iowa. They're real estate agents in the

GROWIN' MORE THAN VEGGIES. Traci gets help in the garden from Jake and Elli—then Elli makes a "pet stop". "I want to teach them all the things I did growing up," says Traci.

GROW UP SWIMMINGLY. "Our daughters are more than sisters—they're close friends from time they spend together here," notes Traci, enjoying splashing around with the kids at their creek.

)P OF COLOR. Sunflowers in an old Pepsi ate add a colorful accent to a flower bed.

DAWN OF A NEW DAY—likely with little time for the hammock. With full-time jobs, plus the farm and their family, Bill and Traci stay busy.

Ames area, and most of the land in Story County is f-l-a-t.

"We live on the only bump in a big flat valley…with tv creeks and 100-year-old trees," says Bill.

The couple bought the building site and 12 acres. Later, th were able to purchase the adjoining 28 acres that had been sp off earlier. "That allowed us to put the farmstead back togethe notes Traci.

Today they have 175 acres of pasture and cropland a run about 75 beef cows. That's in addition to their real esta business.

"The farm is our entertainment," notes Bill. "Everything do there is a good change of pace from the office."

Children's Paradise

It's also a great place to raise their children: Elli, 10, Abby, and Jake, 4.

"We want to teach the kids responsibility, like doing chor and all of the little things I did growing up on a farm—li gardening and how to can," says Traci. "Hopefully they'll pa those things along to their children someday.

"Elli has become quite the little cook. She made black ras berry jam for a 4-H project, and it won a purple ribbon at t county fair.

"Abby is our animal lover…and Jake, he can't get enough his sand pile."

And, of course, there's just something about kids and water the Jennings children spend hours down at the creek.

Bill and Traci built a new farmhouse in 2004, and Traci

ON THE LEVEL. The barn was built in 1890, but it stands as straight as the day it was built…and just needed some siding to look like new aga

Side Note: Joy is the feeling of grinning inside.

LORAL FLURRY. Traci loves to garden and watch things grow and it hows—there are flowers everywhere. She used stones from the cel-ar and foundation of the house they tore down to form flower beds.

NVITING ONE AND ALL. The family's new home sits atop a knoll, nd with its cozy front porch, it says "Welcome" to visitors who drive p the lane. The old farmhouse on the place hadn't been lived in for ears and wasn't even a "fixer-upper", so they started from scratch.

THE GREAT ESCAPE. Bill likes nothing better than to hop on a horse and head out to the pasture to check on the cattle.

THE PEPSI GENERATION. Bill enjoys collecting Pepsi-Cola memorabilia...whic explains the Pepsi signs and vintage bottle crates among the timbers of the bar

PEACEFUL PASTURES. Bill runs about 75 beef cows and feeds out the calves. No wonder he likes to check the cattle—sure is peaceful out here

.L THE COMFORTS OF HOME. The kitchen ght) is as spacious as it is spectacular. And a warm summer day, the screened-in back rch is a comfy place to enjoy a burger.

CK THE HALLS. A Christmas wreath found way to the barn, adding cheer year-round.

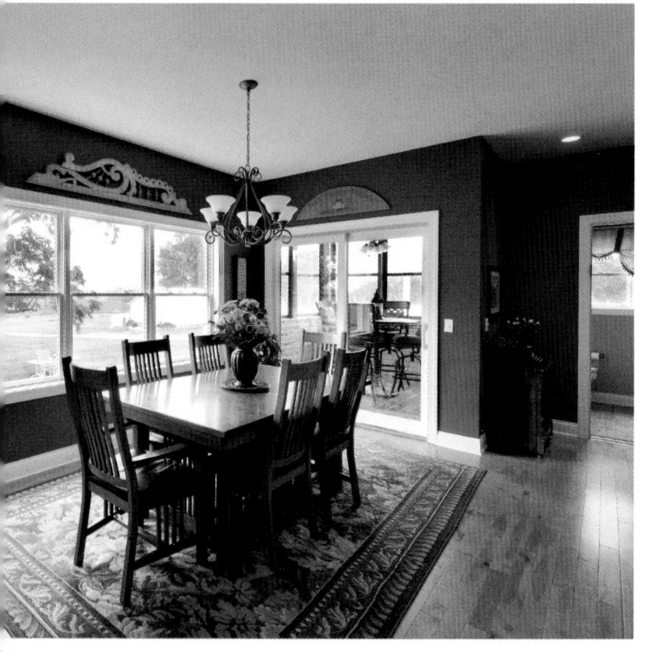

BLE WITH A VIEW. The dining area of the "eat-in" country kitchen s windows—for a view that adds the finishing touch to family meals.

has been adding flower beds ever since. She used stones from the cellar of the old house to form many of the beds.

Gardening Is Great Therapy

"That's my therapy after a busy day," explains Traci. "To buy some plants and then have the kids help plant them—that's really living for me."

Bill's a former biology teacher and loves nature. The beef cow herd keeps him plenty busy, but he readily admits the cows and calves are mostly an excuse to hop on a horse and just enjoy the outdoors.

Who could blame him when those outdoors happen to be on one of the Prettiest Farms in Iowa?

NOTES FROM NOTEWORTHY IOWANS...

"A MAN'S GOT to have a code, a creed to live by, no matter his job." *—John Wayne, actor from Winterset*

"FROM THE STANDPOINT of the road I took—rural development in Third World countries—growing up on a small Iowa farm was the best foundation on which to build my career." *—Norman Borlaug, Nobel Peace Prize winner from Cresco*

Side Note: Promise a lot and give even more.

Young Schoolteachers Learned a Lesson

Gerald Row

The grass wasn't so green on the other side of the fence after all.

By Janine Zantingh, Pella

I'M A PROUD GRADUATE of the University of Northern Iowa. Upon completion of my education, I headed to Des Moines to do my student teaching in 2008.

While residing in our capital city, I met my future husband—a 6-foot-9 basketball player from Dordt College in Sioux Center. We got married among the tulips in Pella and promptly moved to, ahem…Connecticut.

I know what you're thinking—why Connecticut?

Well, it's no small secret that young Iowa professionals are hot commodities nationally—employers everywhere recognize our Iowa work ethic and values. We were no exception and were recruited for positions as Christian schoolteachers in the Constitution State.

Though we told everyone we were moving because of the jobs, the allure of "getting out" played a big role in our decision to relocate to the East Coast. It seems like, for some reason, most of us believe we have something to prove when we graduate—that we can leave and make it elsewhere.

Apparently we weren't paying attention when we were taught that you don't know what you have until you've left it all behind. Must have glossed over that chapter!

Expensive and Unfriendly

We arrived in Connecticut at the end of August, eager to start our new journey together. After settling in to our $1,000-a-month one-bedroom/one-bath apartment (gasp), I headed to the "local" grocery store and found myself in shock. Shock at the gargantuan size of the buildin[g]. Shock at the gargantuan prices for a ga[l]lon of milk or a pound of ground bee[f].

> *"I missed one-handed waves off the steering wheel that Iowans do..."*

Upon finding my way through th[e] maze of unending aisles and making m[y] purchases, I headed for home. On my wa[y] out the door, I stopped to smile at an old[er] woman coming in.

I was raised, like any Iowan, to believ[e] a stranger is just a friend you haven't m[et] yet, so I was not expecting her respons[e]. She narrowed her eyes, tilted her head [to] the side and asked if I knew her.

When I replied that I did not, she th[en] asked why I smiled at her. "Just bein[g] friendly," I said.

With which she promptly answere[d], "Well don't."

I tried to shake off the encounter in th[e] car and look forward to dinner, convinc[ed] that the rude exchange would be a on[e]-time experience. Sadly, this first day w[as] foreshadowing all our days to come.

ALL ROADS LEAD TO HOME...in idyllic Iow[a]. But not so on the traffic-jammed East Coa[st].

Side Note: Daily prayers lessen daily cares.

At home, my husband and I sat down
enjoy the hamburgers he had master-
lly grilled. One bite and we could tell
e weren't in Iowa anymore, as if we
eded more reminding.

Friday Night Ball Games

But it wasn't just the rude people, diculous prices or unpalatable beef that ade me pine for home. I missed the open ace, fields stretching for miles like a atchwork quilt, made of every shade of ch green and earthen brown.

I missed Friday night varsity basket- ll games...and fresh corn on the cob, aded to my grandfather by a farmer for xing his broken backhoe.

I missed passing vehicles on the road d getting that one-handed wave off the eering wheel that Iowans do. Heck, I issed people who knew how to drive!

I missed the things that make Iowa so ecial and different from anywhere else the world.

Left After a Year

As a result, our stint in "greener pas- res" didn't last long. We moved back a ear later with no employment prospects, ut plenty of faith that the Good Lord ould provide, which He did.

With every mile closer to our state bor- er, I felt I could breathe a little easier. he claustrophobic mountains faded into e rearview mirror, and the landscape egan to open up again.

With every corn or soybean field, I new I was getting closer to home. I never ought fertilizer could smell so sweet!

As our wheels rolled across the bridge panning the Mississippi River, tears arted flowing down my cheeks. I had ever seen anything so beautiful as that Welcome to Iowa" sign.

I proudly proclaim Iowa as my home gain. My husband and I now have a hance to raise our children on corn on e cob, Friday night games and strang- rs who believe you are just a friend they aven't met yet.

The Old Farmer Sez...

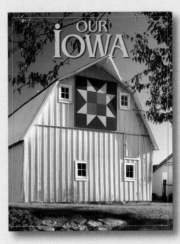

Have a favorite saying? Send to: "Side Notes", Our Iowa, 1606 Golden Aspen Drive, Suite 109, Ames IA 50010.

Buffalo Still Roam This Iowa Prairie

Join us as another reader takes us for a drive along his favorite rustic roads.

Story and Photos by Lynn Betts

NEXT TIME you're in the Sioux City area, take a drive north on Highway 12 to the Broken Kettle Grasslands Preserve. It's a place like no other in Iowa.

For starters, at *4,000* acres, Broke Kettle is Iowa's largest remaining nativ prairie. It's the only place you'll find pra rie rattlesnakes and nesting magpies. An it's the site of the first bison birth in Iow in more than 150 years.

The nine bison calves that roam th prairie with a herd of 28 older bison brin to mind visions of the Great Plains of ye

HALLOWED HILLS. Mandan and Pawnee Indians once hunted buffalo—and even grew corn—her Some of their unearthed pottery led to the name Broken Kettle, says manager Scott Moats (left

THE WAY IOWA USED TO LOOK...with buffalo grazing the native prairie grasses of the Loess Hills... and even rattlesnakes amid the wildflowers on places like Rattlesnake Knob (below). Scott says the best way for him to get around the 4,000-acre preserve is by horseback or with a four-wheeler.

Side Note: Men trip not on mountains; they trip on molehills.

eryear. As a matter of fact, that's what preserve manager Scott Moats likes best about this landscape gem in northwest Iowa—the vastness of it all.

"The sheer size of Broken Kettle is what's most impressive to me," says Scott. "It's large enough to let your imagination wander. And it changes every day and every season."

Over 150 Bird Species

That change comes about because of the more than 200 species of plants and 150 different bird species on the preserve.

"That's why the bison are here," Scott explains. "I couldn't tell you how far they walk in a day, but I do know they'll cover the entire pasture each day, eating the plants that are most succulent that day.

"The way they roam and pick and choose plants brings more biodiversity to our prairie. We hope to build the herd to 250 at some point."

If you visit, it's not a sure thing you'll see the bison—the 500-acre bison pasture is off-limits to visitors. But there's a pretty good chance you might see the herd from a distance from Butcher Road.

Butcher Road winds its way from the flatland a few miles south of Westfield along the Missouri River floodplain... then through steep, rugged terrain...to one of the ridgetops of Iowa's famed Loess Hills.

"You can appreciate the expanse of the prairie from there, and on a clear ⮕

THEY REALLY DO ROAM. Buffalo walk miles and miles looking for the most succulent plants each day. Guess that makes them "picky eaters"

WILDFLOWERS like this yellow flax are among 200 plant species in the preserve.

day, you can see 25 miles—all the way to Vermillion, South Dakota," says Scott.

Visitors can hike on the south side of Broken Kettle. The preserve's headquarters has an outside kiosk with maps. Don't expect tours or to even find someone at headquarters all the time, though.

The preserve is owned by The Nature Conservancy. "Our purpose is to promote biodiversity, not to offer public recreation," Scott explains, "so there are no hiking trails, and you're pretty much on your own.

"But we do want to do what we can to share this rich prairie with people."

About Those Rattlesnakes...

You'll likely find the purple coneflower, pasqueflower, little bluestem, yucca and other native prairie plants on your hike, and you may hear coyote howl at sundown.

The prairie is also home to badgers, bobolinks, the Great Plains toad, and prairie butterflies like the regal fritillary and Pawnee skipper.

And the rattlesnakes?

"We first saw the prairie rattlesnak here in 1999. We probably have some where over 200 of them now. I'd gues I could go out to Rattlesnake Knob mos any day I wanted and find one," replie Scott.

NOTES FROM NOTEWORTHY IOWANS...

"I STARTED to analyze what it was I really knew...it was Iowa. Suddenly I realized that all the really good ideas I'd ever had came to me when I was milking a cow. So I went back to Iowa (from France)." *—Grant Wood painter from Anamosa*

"BEING a politician is a poor profession. Being a public servant is a noble one." *—Herbert Hoover 31st President of the U.S. from West Branch*

Side Note: "To me, a lush carpet of pine needles or spongy grass is more welcome than the most luxurious Persian rug." —Helen Keller

CHURCH ON THE RIVER

Sitting in a canoe instead of a pew, he discovered a special place to reflect.

By Dale Mills, Cerro Gordo County Hawk-Eye

LIKE AN ALTAR to the Creator, limestone bluffs rise from the Upper Iowa River...inspiring as the Winnebago, where the author canoes.

QUIET and serene, the inky-black waters of the Winnebago River greeted me before the sun's rays broke through the early morning sky. Venus was bright as a diamond, reflecting the sun I would not see for another hour.

We're blessed to live along the Winnebago here in Cerro Gordo County, and I go canoeing every chance I get—sometimes, like today, on Sunday mornings before church.

Raging floodwaters of 2008 had caused massive property damage and heartache here. But on this early morning, the river valley was veiled in silence and peacefulness...and as I settled into my canoe, it felt similar to being the first to enter an empty church sanctuary.

A great blue heron served as the greeter. But rather than usher me downstream a couple hundred yards at a time like herons usually do, it immediately turned and flew upstream over me. It seemed dumbfounded by my presence.

Cardinal's First Hymn

Around the next bend, a cardinal started his morning song. Using the best cardinal imitation I could muster, I joined in a responsive liturgy, though I silently wondered if I was courting or cursing him in his language.

> "Like incense, the scent of bergamot tickled my nose..."

Soon a blue jay, singing way out of tune, disrupted and silenced our special music.

A second and then third heron stood motionless near the bank, no doubt looking for breakfast. Both noisily scolded me for the second hymn of the morning. I felt like squawking back at them but decided to stay in tune with my surroundings.

A bit farther downstream, I found myself looking heavenward at the topmost branches of the tallest cottonwood trees. The leaves up there shimmered a golden iridescence in the first rays of the sun on this Sunday morning.

Distracted by the sight of the leaves when I should have been giving the river the attention it required, my canoe loudly scraped the stream bottom. Amid the silence all around me, it was akin to an unruly child making noise in the middle of a prayer.

The rocks grated the bottom of my canoe—sounding worse than it really was, much like that child's temper tantrum during the prayer. The river soon deepened and quieted the squall, just as parents would take care of an insubordinate youngster.

The fresh light of dawn was now filtering through the trees, much like sunshine streaming through stained glass. In this soft light, I could see a doe and speckled twins. Not one so much as blinked an eye as I floated by.

Raccoons Scurried Up a Tree

A mother raccoon and two babies ambled close to the water's edge, probably tired from an evening of merrymaking. Farther downstream, two more raccoons scurried up a tree. Possibly just weaned, they stopped on a branch and tried to look big... quietly hissing and puffing themselves up in an attempt not to be scared.

Like incense, the pungent scent of wild bergamot tickled my nose. Overhead, a red-tailed hawk sassed me.

Upon approaching a still backwater, I listened to what sounded like hogs at a trough filled with soaked shell corn. The sound grew louder as I drew near, and I saw not hogs, but a school of carp with their large mouths sucking at the water surface.

A slap of the paddle, and carp wakes exploded in every direction. I had to chuckle—it looked like rambunctious youngsters rushing out of Sunday school.

An hour had passed since I first put in to the river. My spirit was refreshed, and now it was time to leave this sacred place and head home for breakfast...and then on to church for the "second service".

Side Note: Going to church doesn't make you a Christian any more than standing in a garage makes you a car.

IO-WAYS

Featuring a summertime photo tour of our byways and backroads.

Summer in Iowa is simply sense-sational. And it's more fun than fireworks at the county fairgrounds on the Fourth of July!

Red barns and colorful flowers look especially brilliant ;ainst the backdrop of green fields and blue skies. And you've ever smelled freshness until you've inhaled the Iowa country r after a thundershower.

It's a barefoot time of year...a time to seek the coolness of 1 old maple tree in the heat of the day. Strawberries are ripe for e pickin', and it won't be long before that first juicy tomato of e season will be ready for slicing.

We work with some of the top professional photographers Iowa, who travel the backroads from the Missouri to the Mississippi to bring you the sights of summertime in our state.

So pour a cold glass of lemonade and join us for this issue's photo tour.

LIFE IN THE SLOW LANE. Beware of tortoises (and a few hares) on Frenchtown Road in Clayton County.

Joseph Stanski

BLOOM WHERE YOU ARE PLANTED. So says an old adage, and these black-eyed Susans are doing just that...creating quite a backyard bouquet.

ARGING ONTO THE SCENE is a powerful tugboat pushing its tow against the current of the mighty Mississippi River at Pikes Peak State ırk near McGregor. At left, a creek (also known as a kid's paradise!) meanders through the fertile farmlands near Paullina in O'Brien County.

This photo and below: Gerald Rowles

Don Poggensee

ALL EARS AND LEGS. But these foals w
soon grow into their bodies and be ready
work Amish farm fields in Buchanan Count

FEAST FOR THE EYES...and the honeybee
But pity the bees—they won't know where
go first in this flower bed in Jasper Count

OUT OF THE BLUE flow the waters of the Volga River in Fayette County. Canoeing the Volga is popular—and with such beauty, it's easy to see wh

HE ROAD LESS TRAVELED is a good place to be on a summer's day in Harrison County. Who knows what sights await around the bend. So let's go!

Howard Vrankin

LEARING AFTER THE STORM. An old corncrib basks in the soft, late-afternoon light fter a passing thundershower. Farmers call timely summer showers "million-dollar rains".

Don Poggensee

HITTING THE SHOWERS—or the ol' swimming hole—after a spirited mud volleyball contest in Lake View.

KISSED BY THE SUN. Backlit by the lat
afternoon sun, tree leaves seem to shimm
as they are reflected in a quiet pool at bea
tiful Ledges State Park in Boone Count

OW'D YOU LIKE to be in the same boat as these guys? Crawford Creek in Ida County looks like a great spot to while away a sunny summer afternoon.

Don Poggensee

LILIES OF THE ALLEY is what one wag we know calls hollyhocks because they're so common. Common or not, it's not summer without Grandma's pretty blossoms.

ANCIENT ARCHITECTURE. This old corncrib looks a bit like an Oriental pagoda silhouetted by the sunrise. Then again, you won't find many pagodas in Carroll County!

WONDER BUD. Indians used purple coneflower for snakebite, anthrax and pain relief, and modern medicine men say it cures the common cold. Maybe so, but mostly we think they're pretty!

Marty Hulsebos

WOULDN'T BE SUMMER in Iowa without a meadowlark perched on a post and with a song in his hea

Don Poggensee

THERE'S LIGHT AT THE END OF THE TUNNEL...and fittingly, it's the heavenly Iowa sunshine along a tree-canopied country road in Ida Coun

Gerald Rowles

OOD HAYMAKING WEATHER. Pushed along by a high-pressure system, these fluffy white ouds appear to be racing to the far horizon in Marion County. The light breeze and low umidity combine for a perfect day for chores like baling hay...or maybe just playing hooky!

Gerald Rowles

Julie Habel

UMPING FOR THE JOY OF IT. Wouldn't it be fun to be a kid again, like these hay-bale-hopping youngsters...but only if you grow up in Iowa! The quality of life here can't be beat.

ING OF WINGS. Iowa is home to over 100 species of butterflies—many quite colorful. ut it's hard to beat a monarch for regal beauty. It's appropriately named, don't you think?

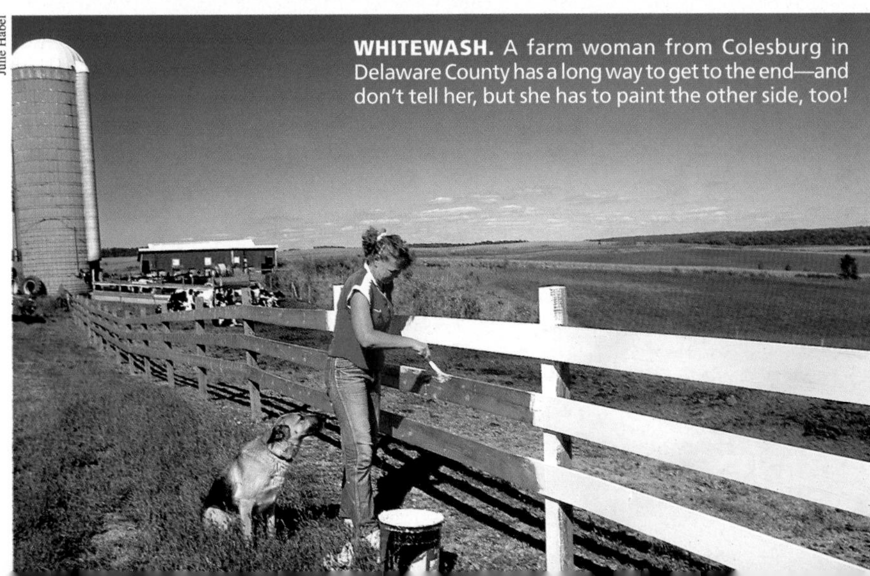

Julie Habel

WHITEWASH. A farm woman from Colesburg in Delaware County has a long way to get to the end—and don't tell her, but she has to paint the other side, too!

IT'S A BERRY GOOD DAY...when strawberrie are ripe for pickin'! Strawberry shortcake, anyone

Don Poggensee

Ty Smedes; next page: Joseph Stanski

THEY DON'T BUILD 'EM LIKE THIS ANYMORE. Potter's Mill was built way back in the 1840s in Bellevue. Restored as a bed-and-breakfast, the gristmill ground flour until 1969.

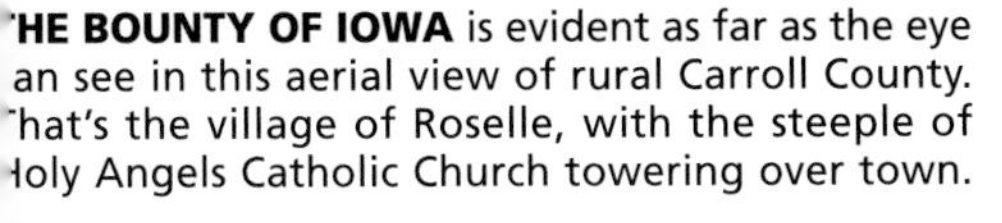

'HE BOUNTY OF IOWA is evident as far as the eye an see in this aerial view of rural Carroll County. 'hat's the village of Roselle, with the steeple of ioly Angels Catholic Church towering over town.

T'S THRESHING TIME! These oat shocks will soon e hauled from the field for threshing on an Amish arm in Washington County. It's hard, hot work, but lso exciting as neighbors gather together to help ach other. And oh, those threshing dinners at noon!

URN THE PAGE to catch the last rays of day in efferson County. The old barn stands empty, but kely still echoes with sounds of the evening chores.

THAT CONCLUDES our photo tour of summerime in Iowa. Thanks for coming along! And join s for more seasonal sensations on pages 54 and 74.

Joseph Stanski

The Prettiest Farm in Iowa

BEAMING TEAM. You'll find Mary Lou Egeland managing the tiling office every day while Doug is on location supervising the work crews.

Nothing symbolizes our state like proudly primped and painted farmsteads. We showcase one of the prettiest in each issue.

Story and Photos by Denny Eilers

NOT too many years ago, this issue's "Prettiest Farm" was a fa cry from pretty.

The house and barn needed repair, as well as gallons an gallons of paint. A tornado had rippe through, damaging the trees. Debris wa everywhere.

"Everything needed to be fixed," recal Doug Egeland.

The farm was one of four that had bee given to Luther College by an area farmer when he passed awa

A FIXER-UPPER...that Doug and Mary Lou fixed up pretty as you please. The house and barn were the only buildings worth saving when they bought the farm 15 years ago—and they needed lots of work and gallons of paint. Plus, a tornado had downed trees and scattered debris everywhere.

t the age of 91. Luther decided to sell them at auction.

"That's when we got interested," says Doug's wife, Mary ou. "We saw the ad in the paper. It was close, so Doug and I rove over several times to check it out.

"We imagined what it could be. There was a spring on the rm, and we envisioned a nice pond there someday."

Run a Successful Farm Business

The Egelands got their start as dairy farmers but transitioned to a drainage tiling business more than 30 years ago.

"I wanted to quit milking," Doug recalls. "Mary Lou was aching school, coming home and milking cows after school. Ve decided we wanted to do something else."

Doug started as a one-man band with just a backhoe. The usiness grew and today operates with the latest equipment, staff of eight, and covers an 80-mile radius from the Ossian ome base.

Doug and Mary Lou's story goes back even further than that. the 10th grade, they became high school sweethearts...about e time Doug had purchased a tractor and began custom- ⇒

RECYCLED. An old bulldozer accents a flower bed...while a boulder in the yard with the Egeland name adds a sense of permanence.

LOOKS TWICE AS NICE reflected in the spring-fed lake. Mary Lou designed the gazebo and footbridge, and Doug built them—but not without a little excitement. He was ferrying lumber to the island when his skid-steer loader broke through the ice. *Brrrr!*

THE EAGLE HAS LANDED in the yard—one of man surprises. There's even a guest cabin (below) by the lake

OUT OF THE WOODS comes Doug on his ATV. A to nado had wiped out the farm's trees, so the Egeland planted 5,000—and now sell them for transplanting

Side Note: Ever stop to think, and forget to start again?

AKE A GANDER at this water garden along the lane, then turn the page for a dramatic view of the lake lit up for an evening of entertainment. ↳

›plying nitrogen fertilizer for farmers in the area.

He missed a lot of school, and to cover for him, Mary Lou rote excuse notes—until the principal caught on. He told Doug, The way you're going, you won't amount to anything but a tch digger."

Doug shared that story when he gave his high school's com-encement address years later, quipping, "The principal was ght—but I never knew how much money there was in digging tches!"

Turned Dream into Reality

Back to the farm: The Egelands purchased it in 1995 and nmediately started their own "Farm Makeover: Extreme dition".

The first step was taking out all the fences. "With no fences, e couldn't have any livestock," Doug says with a smile.

The 3-acre pond was created in 1995-96, with help from e Egeland tiling crew. It took about a year to fill with pringwater.

Next, Mary Lou designed the pond's gazebo, with a bridge ading to it. That winter Doug was hauling lumber for the gazebo ross the ice, when his skid-steer loader dropped through, and found himself sitting in 5 feet of icy water. "I got out of there a hurry, but we had to lift out that loader with a crane," says oug.

The buildings and pond are surrounded by 5,000 hardwood d spruce trees. "A hobby that got out of hand," explains Mary ou.

In fact, they've transformed their love of trees into a busi-ess—they sell and transplant for customers, using a large tree spade. "We only work with large trees—that's our niche," notes Doug. "Many people don't want to plant a small tree and wait for it to grow."

Backdrop for Graduation Photos

With its endless supply of backdrops—gazebo, bridge, light-house and more—the farm has become a favorite with local photographers for senior high school pictures.

Mary Lou and Doug have also hosted weddings, family reunions and other gatherings. In 2000, they celebrated the 25th anniversary of their farm tiling business by hosting a 2-day open house for customers.

"We had over 1,200 visitors," says Mary Lou. "It really sur-prised us—they came from all over. We had a dance band, hot-air balloon rides and a lot of food."

They've also hosted special fund-raisers for families who have been hit with expenses from costly illnesses…proving that the beauty of this Prettiest Farm is more than skin-deep.

NOTES FROM NOTEWORTHY IOWANS…

"I COULD PROVE God statistically. Take the human body alone. The chances that all the functions of an individual would just happen is a statistical monstrosity."
—George Gallup, pioneering pollster from Jefferson

"I DIDN'T HAVE to make up anything for *The Music Man*. All I had to do is remember." *—Meredith Willson creator of the Broadway hit from Mason City*

Side Note: We only learn our limits by going beyond them.

'Wild Turkeys Skittered Across The Road in Front of the Buggy'

Sunday Diary Entry: "Our horse 'Rita' was a little skittish at first, but then trotted calmly on."

Side Note: Real abundance is found when we join hands with the ones we love.

WARM GREETINGS from our Amish community in Davis County.

I'm Ruby Kuhns, and I keep a week-long diary of life on our family farm. My husband, Jacob, and I have 11 children: Kathryn, 18, Rosalyn, 17, Edna Marie, 16, Paul Harvey, 14, Regina, 13, Galen, 11, Wilbur, 9, Loren, 7, Matthew, 4, Luke Allen, 2, and Jeremy, 1.

We have a 170-acre dairy farm. Plus we sell baked goods May through October at the farmers markets in Muscatine and Davenport, and during the summer in Bloomfield. During the peak of the season, we'll bake well over 100 pies, plus cakes, cookies and rolls on Thursdays and Fridays in our basement.

My parents live down the road a few hundred yards from us, and they've had a bit of bad news since my last diary. Mom has had cancer twice in the past 2 years, and they went to Mexico for a checkup in September.

The checkup showed the cancer has returned. They stayed in Mexico for 4 weeks while she received chemo treatments. The plan is to return later for her final treatment. Meanwhile, we're glad to have them back home.

Many prayers have gone heavenward that Mom may be cured, but we know it's in God's hands.

Sunday, Oct. 16 (2011): We didn't have church in our district today. So we took advantage of the free morning to sleep in a bit. But while Jacob and the boys were still choring, Kathryn and Rosalyn left for church at a friend's home in another district.

> *"I guess we almost bit off more than we could chew today..."*

The rest of us spent the morning relaxing. Loren read to Matthew and Luke Allen from a Bible storybook.

At about 1 o'clock, we left for Sunday school at Harley Kauffman's house. On our way over, a few wild turkeys skittered across the road in front of us. Our buggy horse "Rita" was a little skittish at firs but then she trotted calmly on.

At Sunday school, we sang a fe songs, then read two chapters out of tl New Testament. Today we studied Tit chapters 1 and 2.

The younger children also have class in which they're taught to read the Germa language, since we read the Testaments German.

We stopped at Mom and Dad's on t way home. Mom didn't attend Sunda school—she needs to avoid crowds s as not to pick up any flu bugs while h immune system is so run-down from t chemo. She also tires very easily.

Supper consisted of hot tomato sou and tomato sandwiches. The hot sou tasted good on such a chilly day. Fee like winter is just around the corner.

Monday, Oct. 17: Jacob had a b

FOR RELIGIOUS REASONS, Amish adul don't wish to have close-up photos take of themselves. We're honoring that by n photographing our diarist. Instead, we' showing scenes of what you'd see whi driving through Iowa's idyllic Amish countr

y planned, so he was in a hurry. He anted to begin harvesting Dad's corn, t first had some machinery to repair. It's egina's week to help with barn chores, t Kathryn went out, too, to speed up the ilking.

I do all of our bookkeeping and worked n that before breakfast. Edna Marie sorted undry and fixed breakfast while Rosalyn cked lunches for the schoolchildren.

After breakfast, the children left for hool with Rita hitched to the open buggy. hey're usually eager to go because they ke to play softball before school starts.

Our children go to a one-room schoolouse 1-1/2 miles from our farm. A total f 33 pupils attend, and we have two achers for all eight grades.

I have two brothers and a sister whose ildren also attend this school. So 18 of

By dark, the girls had picked 25 big pails of tomatoes..."

e pupils are Dad's grandchildren!

I caught a ride with the schoolchilen to the neighborhood phone booth. walked home, stopping at Mom's for a sit.

Kathryn did Grandma and Grandpa's undry, while Rosalyn did ours. Edna arie took care of the small boys, washed shes and fixed lunch. Jeremy was feelg out of sorts, so that consumed a lot of er time.

I worked on a big pile of mending—ostly denim pants—and promptly after nch went to Ottumwa to check on some bels we'd ordered from a printing shop ere. Both Hy-Vee grocery stores in ttumwa have ordered pies from us, and e needed labels by tomorrow.

I proofed the labels and made some hanges, and while the labels were eing printed, I did some shopping. I ropped them off at home, then took off r Rutledge, Missouri to get some pie omes. I'd ordered them from our wholeale supplier last week, but they were out f stock. So I had to get them before we repared the Hy-Vee order tomorrow.

I didn't get home from Rutledge until :15 tonight. While I was gone, Edna larie and her cousin Sara did some of randma's fall yard work. They raked aves, planted tulip bulbs and dug elehant ears to store for the winter. They lso dug sweet potatoes and winterized er flower beds.

Meanwhile, Kathryn dug our sweet potatoes and regular potatoes. We had a nice crop in spite of the fact that we had to replant in July because of the weather.

Jacob and Paul Harvey worked on machinery repairs all day and are now ready to start harvesting Dad's corn tomorrow.

All and all, it was a busy day.

Tuesday, Oct. 18: Kathryn and Regina helped the boys with the chores and milking, so Jacob could make preparations for harvesting corn and harness the horses.

After breakfast, everyone scattered in different directions. Jacob and Paul Harvey went out to the field. Kathryn cooked the pie filling for that Hy-Vee order—as well as an order for 19 pies we got yesterday from CJ's Restaurant in Bloomfield.

After lunch, Kathryn went up to Grandpa's to bring in and fold their laundry, while Rosalyn, Edna Marie and I worked on the pies. Our quiet afternoon peace was broken when I heard the clatter of shoes and lunch boxes upstairs as the children came home from school.

I was happy for the help, though. Galen and Wilbur helped Kathryn mix feed and do the chores. Loren straightened the house and entertained the small boys, then went out to the barn to help with the milking.

I sent the other three girls to haul in the potatoes and some pumpkins, since there was a chance of frost tonight. They also picked some tomatoes.

We grew an open-pollinated variety, and the plants didn't set fruit until late summer. They're just now beginning to ripen. By dark, the girls had picked 25 5-gallon pails.

Some of the tomatoes were huge—the largest one weighed 2-1/2 pounds and measured 17-1/2 inches around!

Edna Marie also pulled up all of the geraniums by the roots and put them in a box in the basement. Early next spring, I'll trim off the dead branches and pot them. Most of them will grow again.

Jacob and the boys helped us when they came in from choring. Good thing, because we were running late with our pies.

I guess we almost bit off more than we could chew today. But it felt good to have so many jobs done.

Wednesday, Oct. 19: A cold windy morning, and the first thing I did was start a fire in our wood-burning stove.

Jacob left for the barn with a lantern. The barn looks cozy and friendly with the light from the lantern shining out the barn windows.

While Kathryn, Regina and the boys were out doing chores, Rosalyn helped me straighten up in the house. With so many small children, there are always things to put away. But I want to enjoy the children now because there'll come a time when the house will be clean and quiet. Then I'll miss the clutter and racket.

After breakfast and devotions, Paul Harvey and Jacob headed for the cornfield with the horses and picker.

I'd arranged for a local taxi driver

Side Note: God gave us memories so we might have roses in December.

Don Poggensee

SCHOOL'S OUT FOR THE DAY...and as the shadows begin to lengthen, these scholars are heading home to do chores. Amish children typically go to school from first through eighth grade.

YOU'LL BE FEELING YOUR OATS with a hearty helping of Ruby's homemade granola.

Ruby's Homemade Granola

18 cups old-fashioned oats
1 pound raw sunflower seeds
4 cups coconut
2 cups wheat germ
2 cups oat bran
1 cup dry milk
1 tablespoon baking soda
1 tablespoon salt
1 cup butter
1/2 cup vegetable oil
2 teaspoons vanilla extract
3 cups brown sugar

In a large baking pan or roasting pan, mix the oats, sunflower seeds, coconut, wheat germ, oat bran, dry milk, baking soda and salt. Melt together the butter, oil, vanilla and brown sugar; pour over dry ingredients and mix well. Toast in the oven.

to pick me up at 9 so I could deliver the pies to the grocery stores in Ottumwa. By the time I got home, the girls had the other pies ready for the restaurant in Bloomfield, so I delivered them as well. While I was in town, I ran some errands and didn't get home until mid-afternoon.

While I was running those errands, Kathryn canned 24 quarts of tomato soup. Edna Marie washed dishes, made yogurt and fixed lunch. Rosalyn folded and put away the laundry that didn't get tended to yesterday.

After lunch, Dad spelled Jacob in the cornfield so he could do some odd jobs around the farm. But first they hitched two more horses to Paul Harvey's team—he was hauling in the loads of corn, and the

> "The barn looks cozy with the lantern light shining in the windows..."

weight was almost too much for the two horses he had been using.

When I got home from town, I picked 10 more pails of tomatoes before supper. I went out again later and picked some more, and altogether, we picked 47 5-gallon pails.

I couldn't find any more buckets, so I just quit. I felt a bit wasteful leaving the rest out there, but I'd picked most of the ripe tomatoes and the largest of the green ones.

Once the work was done, Edna Marie and Rosalyn took some milk and eggs to Grandma for breakfast tomorrow morning. Jacob heard them chuckling as they were coming back up the lane. Evidently, Grandpa told them some funny stories!

Thursday, Oct. 20: I looked out the window first thing this morning and was delighted to see the twinkling of the stars. It's been cloudy every day since Saturday.

Kathryn and Regina had the first load of laundry on the line as the first streaks of dawn appeared in the east. Soon the sun rose bright and clear.

I couldn't help but think of the Bible verse "This is the day the Lord hath made; we will rejoice and be glad in it." We wouldn't appreciate these nice days as much if we didn't have cloudy days, too.

Today was "bake day" for Saturday's farmers markets, and I mixed cookie dough before breakfast. Edna Marie fixed sandwiches for the children's lunches before starting the cookie baking. Rosalyn swept the house and fried eggs for breakfast.

After breakfast, Rosalyn finished the lunches, putting in a slice of peach pie and some milk. By then, Galen had Rita hitched and the children were off to school.

Jacob and Paul Harvey headed to the field again—on a good day they can harvest 12 acres of corn—while we continued our baking. It took Edna Marie all morning to bake and bag all of the cookies.

After another batch of cookie dough, I made the angel food cakes—just seven of them today, since the markets have really slowed down.

We took time to relax over the noon hour, then I cut up two pails of tomatoes for ketchup. I mixed them with salt and put them in a stockpot, where they'll stay for 5 days. I've never made ketchup before and am eager to try some different recipes.

After school, Regina took the buggy up the road to fetch Grandma. She needed some food out of our locker and also came in for a while to visit. It was go having her at our house again, even if f just a short time.

Regina then gave her a ride to t phone booth and drove her home.

We try to have supper at 5 every ev ning. It can take a while, since everyo has stories to relate about the day, esp cially the schoolchildren. It gets rath noisy when several are talking at the sa time.

After supper, we all had chores do. Regina took Jeremy outside in t stroller to watch Jacob and the boys mi The other girls tackled the never-endi piles of laundry and dishes, then me sured out the flour for making pie dou tomorrow.

When Jacob came in for the night, settled into his recliner. Luke Allen a

TEAMWORK. While Dad heads off with t team, these youngsters are running so walnuts through a hand-crank corn shell

Side Note: Solitude is a good place to visit but a poor place to stay.

eremy were immediately at his side with books, so he told them stories.

My recliner felt extra good tonight. I was tired and rather sore from picking tomatoes last night.

Friday, Oct. 21: The insistent beep, beep, beep of the alarm woke me at 4 a.m. It was hard to get out of my cozy, warm bed—but it was time to wake the girls and start baking pies.

By breakfast, we had a good start on our pies and Jacob had already shoed "Topper" since he wanted to use him today.

Pie-baking went smoothly since we didn't have quite so many today—just 53 large pies and 60 small ones. My niece Treva, who has been helping us the past several weeks, was here again today to lend a hand.

After lunch, we baked rolls and bread. We only have 1 more week of baking for the markets, then we'll be done for the year. We're all ready for a break.

Later in the day, I gave Wilbur, Luke Allen and Jeremy haircuts before they had their baths. We're having Communion church services in our district tomorrow instead of Sunday. That's because a neighboring district is ordaining a new minister on Sunday, and the ministers in our district want to attend.

So we did some of our Saturday routine a day early—including baths and some of the Saturday housecleaning.

Saturday, Oct. 22: *Oh, no—is that the alarm already?* That was my first thought when it rang at 2:30.

I woke Rosalyn, Edna Marie and Galen, since they'd be working at the markets today, and the van was scheduled to pick them up, along with baked goods, at 3.

> *"I've never made homemade ketchup before..."*

After they left, Jacob and I went back to bed for an hour, when it was time for chores.

Church started at 9 a.m. We got an early start and Rita trotted leisurely along. Kathryn and Paul Harvey walked the 2 miles.

Our Communion services last the better part of the day. The Bible stories were interesting and so simply told that even the small children could understand. We sang the closing song at 3:30 p.m.

The menfolk weren't in a hurry to go home, so we ladies had a nice visit after the service.

We got home about 5 p.m., and Galen and the girls arrived home from the markets about 15 minutes later. Of course, we all wanted to hear about their day.

We finished our chores early, which made for a relaxing evening—especially since we could anticipate an enjoyable Sunday at home tomorrow reading, writing and napping.

Thus ends another busy week at our farm. We look forward to a slower pace once we are finished with the harvest, baking and canning for the year.

We may think life is difficult sometimes, but when we count our blessings, we find there is no end to the goodness God bestows on us.

May you find all of the blessings He's given you as well! Good-bye until next time.

Julie Habel

BRINGIN' IN THE SHEAVES. A farmer pitches oats shocks onto a bundle wagon...while a youngster seems head over heels driving the team!

Side Note: You can mold a mannerism, but you must chisel character.

There's Beauty Out Your Back Door

Join us as another reader takes us for a drive along his favorite rustic roads.

"AT DAY'S END, the Ocheyedan River reads like an appointment book with tracks of deer, raccoons and pheasants crossing to the other side. Wildflowers dotting the banks are highlighted by summer sunsets."

WHEN Daniel Ruf lived in Colorado, he found plenty of inspir tion for his photography in the western mountains. But when h moved back to Melvin in northwest Iow to farm, he wondered where that inspir tion might come from.

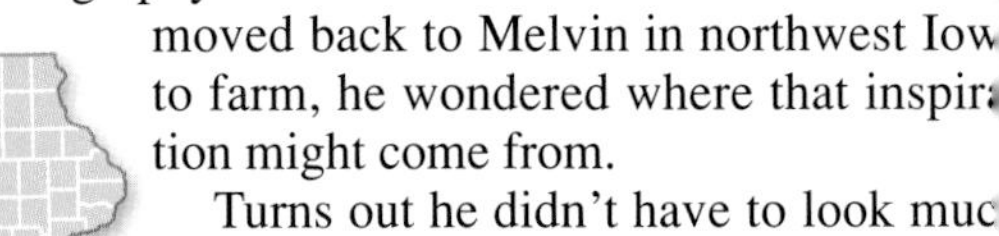

Turns out he didn't have to look muc farther than out his back door.

"Iowa is a land that can be home t both the great bald eagle and tiny sulphur butterfly, a land th grows the tall, stately oak and the wispy big bluestem grass Dan points out. "And all of these wild things make their hom among grazing cattle and sheep and rows of crops that dot th countryside.

"Standing along the banks of the Ocheyedan River, I can fe the Earth's lifeblood as it passes by. A rooster pheasant crow but the soft current of the river continues.

"A white-tailed buck glances for signs of danger, but then di his head for a drink in the cooling waters. The sunlight glin

O BUMP ON A LOG. "Painted turtles wait for no one, and this one as gone as soon as it heard my camera shutter click. The warm sun-ine brings them out to bask for hours at a time on logs in ponds."

cross the river and sprinkles its light across the flowing prairie rasses."

Dan also found inspiration in Iowa's past.

"The history left behind in abandoned barns and farmsteads peaks of a different time, a time of both economic growth and ardships," he notes.

"Quiet barns now, bridles and tack hanging still and brittle on aded walls, a milking pail rusted and overturned in some corner f a cow barn is all that's left of another era. But year after year, e swallows come back to build their nests where the ghosts of past age wander."

NOTES FROM NOTEWORTHY IOWANS...

"IF YOU DO your job well, you'll be successful. If you set out to get rich, you'll never get close." —*Don Lamberti founder of Casey's General Stores from Ankeny*

"WHY CAN'T WE build orphanages next to homes for the elderly? If someone were sitting in a rocker, it wouldn't be long before a kid will be on his lap." —*Cloris Leachman actress from Des Moines*

CALM BEFORE A STORM. "One evening I noticed a storm moving in and grabbed my camera. I was able to capture the magnificence of Iowa."

Side Note: Every sunset is new and exciting...unlike television, there are no reruns.

LIKE A SENTINEL, an abandoned barn and silo resolutely stand watch over the landscape. They echo ith sounds of livestock, and the laughter, tears and dreams of the farm family that worked here."

WINDS OF CHANGE. "Windmills were a necessity—now fodder for photographers."

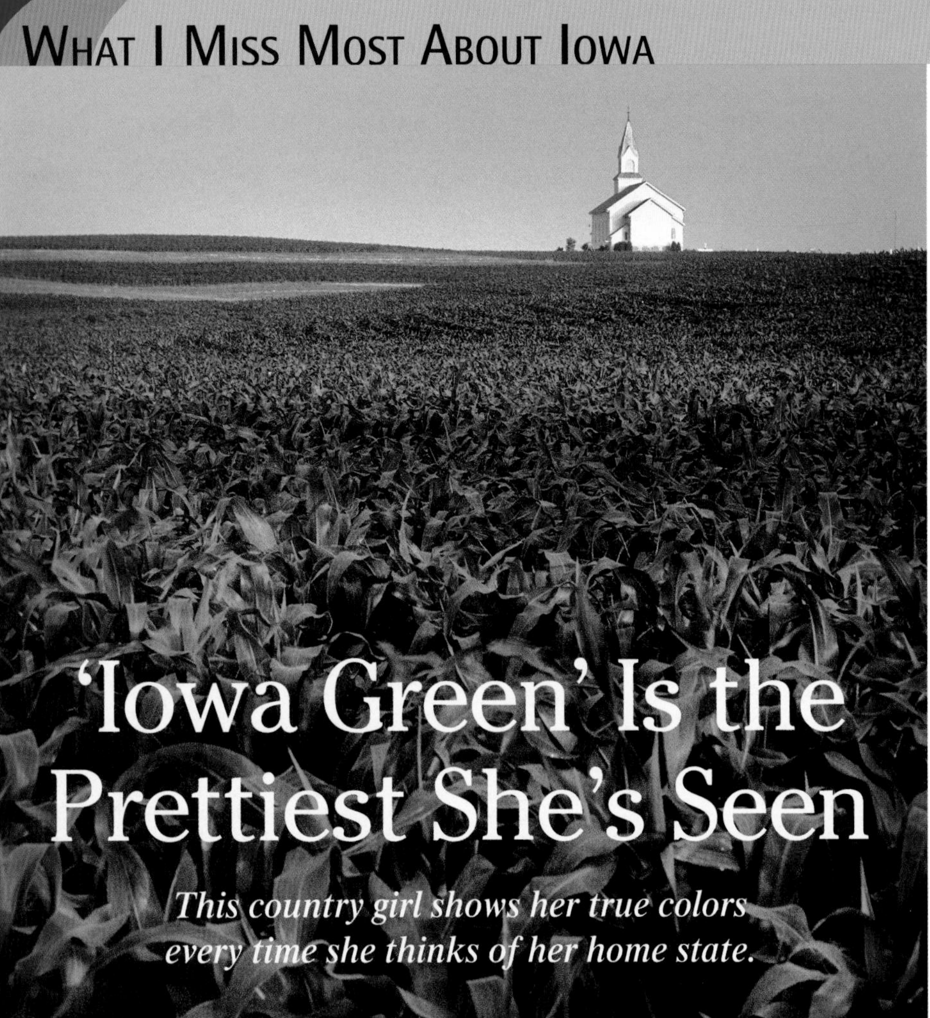

Stephen Gassman

'Iowa Green' Is the Prettiest She's Seen

This country girl shows her true colors every time she thinks of her home state.

By Mildred Hoyd, Boise, Idaho

WITHIN a month of my graduation from Clarion High School in 1960, I was on the road trip of my life.

I found myself traveling from Iowa to Idaho with my second cousin Bettie, her husband, Jack, and their son Tim, who was a year younger than me. It was a journey of 1,500 miles—and I'd never been more than 100 miles from our farm in my life!

> *"Part of me never left Iowa..."*

Bettie and Jack lived in Nampa, Idaho and had come back to Iowa to visit relatives, including my dad, Bob Kirstein. He and Bettie were first cousins and had grown up together.

I felt so grown up! After all, I'd graduated and turned into what I must have thought was a "world traveler". Little did I know that I'd be spending the rest of my life in Idaho. A year after my arrival, Dale and I got married. And after several moves around the state, we settled in Boise, where we've been living the past 46 years.

Rooted in Wright County

A part of me never really left Iowa, though. You see, our family's roots were sunk deep into Iowa's fertile farmland a long time ago. I grew up on the Wright County farm that my great-grandparents homesteaded in 1881.

Dad told me about breaking the tough prairie sod, and of getting his first "town haircut" when he was 12 for Grandpa John's funeral. Mom related stories of prairie fires and Indians.

As for me, there wasn't a better place to grow up in the 1950s than in the middle of Iowa, surrounded by cornfields.

I guess it's human nature to miss most those things that aren't there anymore. My mom and dad and two of my brothers are gone now, and I miss them dearly. Even the buildings on the homestead are gone, replaced by a big steel machine shed. (Thankfully, our family still owns the farm—the land where we were all rooted.)

Beyond that, I miss the color of Iowa—

HEAVENLY HUES. Country church near Gunde overlooks lush fields like the author misse

the greens mostly. Corn green, soybea green, grass green, evergreen green, gar den pea green, tomato plant green, walnu tree green and alfalfa green.

Most folks think green is just one colo but it isn't. Not in Iowa anyway.

There are people who live on the coast who call this "flyover country", and som of them actually confuse Iowa with Idaho If they stopped and took a close look a the many shades of "Iowa green", the wouldn't make that mistake again.

I miss the scents of Iowa, too. The De Moines airport is on the edge of the cit and when I land there, I can get a whiff o productive black soil as soon as the cabi door is opened.

And I immediately smell the humid ity in the air. That's what makes Iow so green—the rich soil and abundar moisture.

Scents and Sounds of Home

I also miss the scent of gravel road dus cow barns and horse stables. In fact, whe I go to the Western Idaho Fair, the firs place I head is to the livestock barns—ju to get my fix of those familiar scents.

I long to hear the sounds of a trac tor pulling into the farmyard. And I mis knowing most everyone I meet when walk down Main Street or into church.

Let's face it, after 49 years away, miss just about everything there is abo Iowa and Wright County—so much s that when I die, I've instructed an Iow nephew to place a perfect ear of corn an a handful of Iowa topsoil on my caske before the grave is closed.

Dale and I have been married 48 year and have three wonderful sons and far tastic grandchildren. Idaho is where the roots are. But maybe some of them wi take a trip like I did someday...and life road will lead them to the place I love s much—Iowa.

Side Note: No one realizes how beautiful it is to travel until he comes home and rests his head on his old, familiar pillow.

The Old Farmer Sez...

"Timing has a lot to do with the outcome of a rain dance."

The Gunderburger!

Go ahead…we dare you to polish off this burger in one sitting!

By Becky Hefel
Clayton County Hawk-Eye

. TRIP to Clayton County in the north-ast corner of Iowa is a delight to the enses…as one beautiful rolling hill fol-ows another through the bluffs and alleys near the Mississippi River.

The breathtaking scenery, friendly lit-e towns and slower pace of life all add) the charm of the area commonly known as Iowa's "Little Switzerland".

When a feast for your stomach becomes as important as a feast for your yes, it's time to pull over and stop at The rish Shanti in the tiny hamlet of Gunder.

Gunder is a town of only 28 people, ut The Irish Shanti has put it on the map vith its famous Gunderburger—likely the argest, two-fisted hamburger you've ever een. It features 16 ounces—yup, a whole ound—of top-quality, locally purchased round beef served plain or with a wide rray of toppings, from traditional cheese, nushrooms and tomatoes to jalapenos and orseradish.

Even that description of the burger oes little to prepare you for its gargan-uan size when a waitress lugs it to your able. When it arrives, diners at surround-ng tables are astonished…then can't esist ordering one as well.

> *"Other diners are astonished when they see it…"*

The top half of the bun is so dwarfed y the burger that it bears resemblance to cherry atop an ice cream sundae.

A Belt Buster

The belt-bustin' burger was already menu feature when Kevin and Elsie Valsh, retired nurses, and their son Hans ought The Irish Shanti 5 years ago.

"We did not want to change a thing," ays Kevin. "We made some improve-nents to the building but kept the same taff and menu. When something works, ou stick with it."

Adds Elsie: "The Shanti serves as a gathering place for the community. We get lots of local farmers who come for lunch. It's a good place to see your neighbors."

Gunder is located along County Route B60, which is part of the River Bluffs Scenic Byway. It's a popular route for snowmobilers in winter and motorcycle clubs in summer, and The Irish Shanti is a renowned pit stop along the way.

Seasoned with Hospitality

The Walshes serve up a great deal of hospitality to accompany your meal. Kevin's a Boston native who adds his Irish joviality and East Coast accent to a smattering of Gunder and Irish lore he likes to share. That, along with the great food, draws travelers from all over the country—and brings them back next time they're in the area.

"We want customers to have an experience that is more than just eating," Kevin explains. "We want them to see what hospitality and good service combined with good, homemade food is all about."

Anyone who can eat the Gunderburger in one sitting gets his picture taken with the famous Gunderburger hat. Others (like me and my friends) opt to take part of the burger home…preferring to save room for the impressive and mouthwatering list of homemade desserts.

Besides burgers (there are *average* size burgers, too), the menu features taste treats like fresh pork loin, turkey tenders and rib eye steaks. Then there are such nightly specials as barbecued ribs and fried chicken (like Mom used to make) with real mashed potatoes.

The Shanti also has one of the largest selections of domestic and imported beers in the county; Guinness, of course, is on tap.

Take a drive along the River Bluffs Scenic Byway and enjoy the feast for the eyes served up by Little Switzerland… and the feast for the stomach prepared by this delightful country cafe. Once you do, I can almost guarantee you'll make it part of your itinerary time and again.

JAWBREAKER. You must open mighty wide to sink your teeth into this meal on a bun served by Kevin and Elsie Walsh at The Irish Shanti.

See page 87 to order yours.

Side Note: May the holes in your net be no larger than the fish in it. —Irish blessing

IO-WAYS

Featuring the wonder of winter along our byways and backroads.

We Iowans are a hardy lot, and most of us would miss having four seasons, including winter.

Oh sure, we grumble a bit when the northwest wind ; strong enough to blow your stocking cap from Sioux City clear cross the state to Burlington. But there's also something special bout winter in Iowa.

Maybe it's the quiet of winter we'd miss…the hush of a big-aked, gentle snowfall…the way that snow muffles even your otsteps on a walk through the woods…or the absolute stillness f the winter landscape under the full moon.

It's in stark contrast to the hustle and bustle of the other three easons—a time to ease up a bit, linger over a hot cup of morn-ıg coffee and just take in the quietude.

Some of Iowa's best photographers have captured the essence of winter in our beautiful state. So join us for a photo tour. Better bring your earmuffs, though!

WHITE CARPET of snow on a trail at Saylorville Lake in Polk County (far left) is just too pretty to walk on.

Joseph Stanski

FIRST SNOW of the season gently descends on a park in Jefferson County, where the only sound is a whisper of the wind through the pine boughs.

LURRY OF ACTIVITY as cowboy George Benson from Deep River rounds up the beef cow herd on a cold, snowy day on his farm in Poweshiek County.

Stanley Buman

Gerald Rowles

RECALL THE WINTER OF 2010? It likely too a spring thaw to clear this tractor crossing

"YIKES, THAT'S COLD!" This Canada goos might think twice about sticking around fo winter when his buddies fly south next fall

Denny Eilers

STALKING NEXT YEAR. With this year's cornstalks buried under snow, you can bet planting plans have already begun at this Clayton County farm

HIVER ME TIMBERS! Sunrise at the Freda Haffner Kettlehole Preserve in Dickinson County reveals an overnight dusting of hoarfrost on the trees.

Gerald Rowles

Marty Hulsebos

ON THE COURTHOUSE SQUARE. The courthouse clock tower is a beacon in the night, creating a Currier and Ives scene as snow falls upon Fairfield in Jefferson County.

HANGING ON FOR DEAR LIFE. A lone leaf is one of the last vestiges of fall, adding a splash of color to the otherwise white landscape after a wet snowfall in Madison County.

Julie Habel

FISHING BUDDIES warm the frozen backwaters of the Mississippi near Guttenberg with their smiles. They caught the eye of our photographer hook, line and sinker!

Gerald Rowles

Gerald Rowles

Gerald Rowles

SANTA'S WORKSHOP? This bright red building looks like it could be—except that it's located in Thomas Mitchell Park in Polk County. The 175-acre park is named after the area's first English-speaking settler.

THEY'LL BE BACK SOON. This purple martin house looks forlorn on the frozen landscape, but the martins will return. After wintering in South America, they find their way back to the same nesting site every year.

UNRISE AT SAYLORVILLE. "The windchill was -30° when I ɔok this photo at Saylorville Lake in Polk County," says pho- ɔgrapher Jerry Rowles. "I was chilled to the bone—even ɾith Carhartts and long johns on. But it was all worth it."

TWAS THE DAY AFTER CHRISTMAS...and it sure was a eaut. But Santa spent it washing the soot off his suit. This un photo was taken in a backyard in Dubuque County.

URN THE PAGE and you'll see an Amish buggy heading up ne road on the dawn of Christmas morning in Washington ounty...under a pastel sky that was a gift from Above.

'HAT CONCLUDES our wintertime photo tour. Warm p by turning to page 74, where our photographers take ou down the backroads on a springtime tour of our eautiful land.

Julie Habel; next page: Joseph Stanski

The Prettiest Farm in Iowa

A SPREADING OAK TREE provides a picturesque frame for Mike and Julie Delaney's 1870 farmhouse. Below: Julie, Mike, Meghan, daughter-in-law Michelle and son Michael had visitors arrive for the family photo.

Nothing symbolizes our state like proudly primped and painted farmsteads. We showcase one in each issue.

Story and Photos by Denny Eilers

IF YOU drove by Mike and Julie Delaney's farm some 20 yea ago, you'd have found their well-kept barns and feedlots full beef cattle.

La Motte

But this issue's "Prettiest Farm in Iowa now has a different kind of livestock roam ing its lush Jackson County hills. Th Delaney farm, near La Motte, is home to herd of nearly 80 alpacas.

Baby alpacas are called crias—and for crying out loud, they' cute!

Equally eye-stopping is the farm where they live…with whi board fences bordering the winding lane, special touches an

HEY MOM...SOMEONE'S TAKING OUR PICTURE! A baby alpaca, called a cria, stands close to her mother on a summer day, curiously watching Mike and Julie go about their daily chores.

A TOUCH OF SUMMER COLOR. Brilliant flowers brighten the unique landscaping around the Delaney home. These white hydrangeas are a perfect accent among large rocks and shady trees.

Side Note: No winter lasts forever; no spring skips its turn.

ower beds everywhere, and a massive oak ee on a knoll standing sentinel over it all. Iard telling just how old that spreading oak eally is.

The Delaney farm consists of 180 acres f beautifully rolling pastureland, plus 120 cres of corn and 80 acres of soybeans. Mike ells seed for Pioneer, and Julie worked as a PA for many years before getting into the lpaca business.

"I got tired of sitting behind a desk and vanted to be out in the fresh air and open paces," she says with a big smile.

The Delaneys have three children: Iichael works for John Deere, Meghan

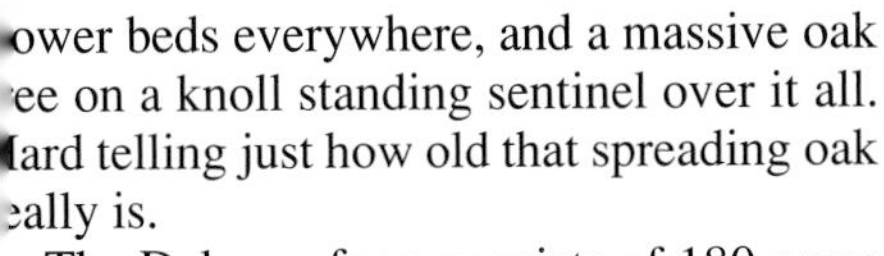

EEING RED. Mike and Julie, members of the owa Barn Foundation, take a lot of pride in eeping their farm buildings well maintained.

Side Note: Your fences need to be horse-high, pig-tight and bull-strong.

THE SKY'S THE LIMIT. A towering oak tree sits atop a knoll overlooking the Delaney farmstead. Who knows how tall this tree might grow

PLAYTIME IN THE PASTURE. Mike and Julie's herd of 80 alpacas spends summer days grazing on 180 acres of rolling Jackson County pasture land. "We no longer had any livestock in the buildings," says Julie, "and we felt our farm was well-suited for something unique like alpacas

TTING PRETTY. The large farmhouse has been remodeled side and out, but still maintains its stately appearance. me sit on one of the porches—there's plenty of room!

RELAX BY THE COOL BUBBLING BROOK. A rock garden and winding brook create a relaxing setting in the backyard. Left: pretty violas add a beautiful splash of color.

tends the University of Iowa and Shannon is doing her doctor's sidency at Harvard.

The family moved to their farm in 1992. Over time, they've modeled the 1870 farmhouse inside and out while maintaining s stately appearance.

An attached garage was added in 2004. The wraparound reened porch and open front porch were completed in 2009.

"Interior additions have been ongoing," says Mike with a rin, "which is typical of an old farmhouse. It never ends."

The house isn't the only building to receive attention. lembers of the Iowa Barn Foundation, Mike and Julie have lso worked hard to maintain their vintage outbuildings…and it ows with white-trimmed red barns at every turn.

Alpacas Were Julie's Idea

You'll still find a few beef cows and calves scattered around e sprawling pastures, but alpacas are taking over.

"Alpacas are herd animals, so you can't buy just one and bring it on your farm," explains Mike.

Alpacas were first imported to the U.S. in 1984 and are now raised throughout North America. They produce one of the world's finest and most luxurious fibers.

Mike was reluctant at first to start raising alpacas, but Julie talked him into it.

"We no longer had any livestock in the buildings," notes Julie, "and I felt our farm was well-suited for something unique like alpacas.

"We were looking for something different that I could take care of."

Mike and Julie didn't jump into their new venture headfirst. They studied the alpaca business for 4 years, then took another 5 years to build up their herd.

"More are now being raised in Iowa," Julie says. "When

Side Note: An open mind opens doors.

READY FOR QUIET TIME. Mike and Julie built this lovely screened-in porch, where they can entertain guests or just unwind after a busy da

A TUB WITH A VIEW. "Interior remodeling has been ongoing since we moved to the farm in 1992, which is typical of an old farmhouse," says Mike.

WARM AND COZY. A beautiful stone fireplace helps warm the spacio living room, a favorite place to spend time when the family gets togeth

we started, there were only five alpaca farms in the state," she says. "Now there are more than 25."

The average Iowa alpaca farm has about a dozen animals, as they can be expensive to purchase. Income is derived from breeding fees and from the sale of offspring and fleece.

Alpacas have a gestation period of 11-1/2 months and are sheared once a year, usually in April or May.

The Delaneys not only raise their own herd, they also board 30 alpacas for other owners who live as far away as Chicago.

Blue-Ribbon Bloodlines

Mike and Julie enjoy belonging to the Alpaca Owners and Breeders Association and travel to shows around the country to meet with other owners. Recently, they won Color Reserve Champion at the Futurity Show in Oklahoma City with one of their male alpacas.

"This is the most competitive show in the country," says Julie, "and having the second-best black male in the country does gre things for our herd and our farm."

The Delaneys also get a blue ribbon for all of their hard wo in making their place one of the Prettiest Farms in Iowa.

NOTES FROM NOTEWORTHY IOWANS...

"IT IS TRUE that I was born in Iowa, but I can't speak for my twin sister (Ann Landers)." *—Abigail Van Buren advice columnist from Sioux City*

"THE SOIL is the mother of man, and if we forget her, life eventually weakens." *—Henry A. Wallace from Orient U.S. Secretary of Agriculture (1933-1940) and Vice President in the Franklin Roosevelt Administration*

Tidbits That'll Wow 'Em at the Coffee Shop

Iere's a host of fascinating facts about our state that are unknown by most Iowans. See how many are news to you.

EVEN IF you were born in Iowa and have lived here all your life, we're betting there are bits of Hawkeye history here you were unaware of before.

For example, did you know that the Rathbun Dam and Reservoir is the largest body of water in the state…that Wright County has the highest percentage of rade-A topsoil in the entire nation…and that Iowa is the only :ate in the U.S. whose east and west borders are 100% formed y water?

That's just the beginning. Here are more facts that may amaze r amuse you:

- Iowa is the only state name that starts with two vowels.
- *Dubuque is the state's oldest city.*
- The state's lowest elevation point—at 480 feet—is in Lee County.
- *Fort Atkinson was the site of the only fort ever built by the U.S. government to protect one Indian tribe from another.*
- Dubuque is home to the only county courthouse with a gold dome.
- *Eagle Grove has an artesian well that has run nonstop for over 100 years.*
- Spirit Lake is the largest glacier-made lake in the state.
- *Sabula is the only town in Iowa that's on an island.*
- The state's smallest city park is situated smack in the middle of the road in Hiteman.
- *Iowa's longest and highest bridge crosses Lake Red Rock.*
- Kalona has the largest Amish community west of the Mississippi River.
- *West Okoboji is state's deepest natural lake at 136 feet.*
- Scranton is home to Iowa's oldest water tower, which is still in service.
- *At 16 miles, East Okoboji is state's longest natural lake.*
- Quaker Oats in Cedar Rapids is the largest cereal company in the nation.
- *Iowa's oldest continually running theater is in Story City.*
- Ripley's Believe It or Not has dubbed Burlington's Snake Alley the most crooked street in the world.

SURROUNDED BY WATER. Sabula proudly points out that it's Iowa's only island town. It's in the Mississippi River 15 miles north of Clinton.

- *In 1967, Amana Refrigeration introduced the first micro-wave—the popular Radarange.*
- Iowa grows three times as much corn as the whole country of Argentina.
- *The highest temperature recorded in Iowa was 118° on July 20, 1934 in Keokuk.*
- Cornell College in Mount Vernon is the only school in the nation to have its entire campus listed on the National Register of Historic Places.
- *The Sergeant Floyd Monument in Sioux City honors the only man to die during the Lewis and Clark Expedition.*
- Iowa's only fire tower is located in Yellow River State Forest.
- *Knoxville's National Sprint Car Hall of Fame and Museum is the only museum in the country dedicated to preserving the history of sprint car racing.*
- Wright County has more artesian wells than any county in the state.
- *The St. Francis Xavier Basilica in Dyersville is the only basil-ica in the U.S. situated outside a major metropolitan area.*
- Of Madison County's six covered bridges, Imes Bridge is the oldest and Holliwell Bridge is the longest.
- *Elkhorn has the largest Danish settlement in the U.S.*
- Crystal Lake is home to a statue of the world's largest bull-head fish.
- *Strawberry Point is home of the world's largest strawberry.*
- The world's highest double track railroad bridge is the Kate Shelley Bridge located in Boone.
- *The Fenlon Place Elevator in Dubuque is the world's steep-est and shortest railway.*
- Francis Drake became Iowa's oldest governor when he was sworn in at the age of 66.
- *The Cedar Rapids Museum of Art houses the world's largest collection of Grant Wood artwork.*
- Iowa is a Native American word for "beautiful land". 

Side Note: If you have a good idea, you need to act on it quickly. Otherwise it's like selling Christmas trees at New Year's.

Iowans' Dream Vacation... Right Here in Iowa

Gerald Row

They spent 10 days touring north of Highway 30—and didn't see it all!

YOU LIVE in Iowa and have 10 days set aside for a vacation... so where are you going to go?

The Rocky Mountains? Hawaiian Islands? A Caribbean cruise?

Not if you're Bob and Shirley Meyer of Denison. A few years ago, this Crawford County couple spent their whole 10-day vacation visiting attractions north of Highway 30 right here in Iowa.

We bumped into Bob at a meeting recently, and he was still talking about the good time they had!

"I was the elementary school principal in Denison (he's since retired), and about the only time my wife, Shirley, and I could take a vacation was in July," explains Bob.

"We wanted to get away for a week or so, but didn't want the hassle of taking a long trip or spend a lot of money. So Shirley and I decided we would take a trip across Iowa, stay north of Highway 30 and see parts of the state we hadn't experienced before. We wanted to explore Iowa and meet new people."

Neither of them are native Iowans—Bob was born in Nebrask and Shirley in South Dakota. After they married in 1963, Bo spent his entire career as an educator in western Iowa.

"We became firmly rooted in the western part of the state, an between my jobs and raising our family, we never had a lot o opportunities to travel Iowa," Bob relates.

"Since the kids had moved away, we thought it was the perfe time to see what was happening in other areas of the state."

> "We had two rules—no fast food and no motel reservations..."

Packed Light—Off They Went!

Bob and Shirley didn't need much time preparing for the trip. They packed a few clothes, grabbed an Iowa Travel Guid headed east to Ames and then north on I-35.

"We had no schedule to follow, and agreed on two rules befor we left: We wouldn't make any motel reservations ahead of tim and we wouldn't eat at any fast-food restaurants," says Bob.

MISSISSIPPI SUNRISE. The morning sun casts a golden glow off the Mississippi River in northeast Iowa (above), one of many breathtaking sights Bob and Shirley Meyer (inset) saw on their Iowa dream vacation.

Side Note: Knowledge in youth is wisdom in age.

"When we got tired at the end of a day, we stayed at the first otel we found that looked clean and comfortable—we didn't ay anywhere very fancy. And we ate at local mom-and-pop staurants that either local residents or people at the motel desk ıggested we try."

And get this—Bob and Shirley found so many interesting aces to visit, they only toured a handful of counties in northeast wa before they had to head back home! So much for seeing the hole northern half of the state.

"As we began our trip, if either of us saw something that terested us, we stopped and looked around," notes Bob.

"We stopped at a few Century Farms that had their plaques ıt by the driveway, just to learn some history of the farm. We so stopped at every church, regardless of the denomination, in ch town we drove through. Iowa is blessed with many beauti-l and interesting churches."

If they arrived in a town and needed directions or information out things to see, they often stopped at a gas station and asked e attendant for advice. Usually this worked, but not always.

"We found it interesting that oftentimes, people living in a mmunity didn't always know about their own local attractions, pecially if they were a little younger," notes Bob.

Discovered Iowa Treasures

Although Bob and Shirley made more stops than they can ven remember, they recall some of the more memorable high-ghts of their vacation:

"Being an elementary educator, I knew one stop I wanted to ake was the Laura Ingalls Wilder Park and Museum in Burr ak," says Bob. "We also enjoyed a stop at the Seed Savers eritage Farm north of Decorah.

"We loved spending time in Winneshiek County. The esterheim Norwegian-American Museum in Decorah was quite teresting. We also ate at two great restaurants in that city."

Everywhere Bob and Shirley stopped, they were greeted by iendly folks who either told them about some of the local his-ry, or made suggestions about additional places to visit after earing about their unique Iowa vacation.

During their stay in Decorah, for instance, a local resident ıggested the Meyers might enjoy driving part of the 109-mile iver Bluffs Scenic Byway, which winds through Fayette and layton counties.

Ty Smedes

OUNTRY TRAVELERS. The Meyers spent a day traveling the quiet ads of idyllic Amish country near Hazleton. "We enjoyed sampling the any homemade goods that the Amish sell at roadside stands," says Bob.

They took this advice and had an enjoyable ride through the pretty countryside known locally as "Little Switzerland"—plus they found many more little towns to visit along the way.

"One of our favorite overnight stops was at The Landing in Guttenberg," recalls Bob. "This beautiful motel was converted from an old pearl button factory years ago. It's located right on the Mississippi River, and the views were spectacular."

Another fun day was spent in Amish country around Hazleton in Buchanan County. Bob and Shirley traveled country roads in the area and enjoyed the idyllic Amish farms and the simplicity of the Amish way of life.

"Since many of the Amish farms have roadside stands where they sell a variety of homemade goods, we enjoyed sampling the fare at several of them," says Bob.

Frank Lloyd Wright Site

They took a memorable tour of the historic home of the late Lowell Walters. Built on a limestone bluff overlooking the Wapsipinicon River at Cedar Rock State Park near Quasqueton, the home was designed by noted American architect Frank Lloyd Wright.

"Mr. and Mrs. Walters were very short in height, and they hired Wright to custom-design this home with their short stature in mind," explains Bob. "All of the furnishings and decor were also designed by Wright. The tour of the home was fascinating."

"We were prepared to come home early if we got bored...never happened!"

They spent an entire day in Dubuque County, visiting the Field of Dreams, the historic Basilica of St. Francis Xavier in Dyersville and the New Melleray Abbey near Peosta, where the monks support themselves by farming and building wooden caskets.

Bob and Shirley also drove through scenic New Vienna, stopping to see the gothic-style St. Boniface Church, known for its awe-inspiring 200-foot-tall steeple.

"Throughout our vacation, we found that Iowans are very proud of their hometowns, and especially their churches," Bob notes.

"While we were at St. Boniface, we found a lady inside who was praying. We started visiting with her when she was finished, and commented that we had also seen the basilica in Dyersville—with its beautiful twin steeples—earlier that day.

"She told us that the church in Dyersville was 'okay', but this church in New Vienna was much nicer," chuckles Bob.

Kids Said They Were Nuts

When Bob and Shirley told their six children they planned to take a 10-day vacation across Iowa, the kids were quite skeptical. "They thought we were really nuts and figured the 'folks' really lost it this time!" Bob says with a laugh.

And admittedly, when the Meyers set out on their trip, they were prepared to come home early if they became bored, tired or ran out of things to do. Never happened!

"Heck, we never even got out of northeast Iowa, there was so much to see and do," says Bob, noting that they might someday like to do a repeat, only south of Highway 30.

"Our vacation reminded us just how beautiful Iowa towns and the rural countryside really are. And the friendliness of the people we met was overwhelming.

"We'd do this again in a heartbeat." 

Side Note: "If you don't know where you're going, you'll end up someplace else." —Yogi Berra

Turkey River Revelry

Bluebells bloom as another reader takes us for a drive along her favorite rustic roads.

Story and Photos by
Joyce Meyer, Spillville

ONE early spring day, Alvin Shindelar drove down to his river-bottom timber, expecting to see tender, new growth of green grass. Instead, he saw a sea of blue—acres upon acres of bluebells blooming in the dappled sunlight on the forest floor.

In all of their years, Alvin and his wife, Edith, had never seen so many bluebells in one spot! The Shindelar farm intertwines with th Turkey River between Spillville and Fort Atkinson in Winneshie County. The landscape is breathtaking...all the more so in sprir when wildflowers make a surprise visit. So delicate, they're he today, and gone in a week or two...although the memory of the lasts much longer.

As Alvin and I walked through his woodland, I smelled th sweet scent of the bluebells, and heard the flow of the Turke River and songbirds in the trees in this quiet, surreal world.

Alvin pointed out the hackberry, oak, walnut and other har woods that grow there. About every 10 years, the Shindelars lo out some of the mature trees and replant with seedlings from th state forest nursery.

It gave me insight into the importance of harvesting ar replenishing the land. I wondered how many beautiful cupboar and coffee tables have been built from the Shindelars' timbe And to see the new trees planted for the next generation is a sig of hope for the future.

May this cycle of life, cheered on by the bluebells of sprin never change.

OUT OF THE BLUE came this sea of bluebells when Alvin Shindelar went to check on his timberland one spring day—more than he'd ever seen there before.

Side Note: A town without trees isn't fit for a dog.

NOTES FROM NOTEWORTHY IOWANS...

"THE SUPPORT I have received from the state of Iowa during my professional career is unmatched. I will always be a proud Iowan." —*Pro golfer Zach Johnson from Cedar Rapids winner of the 2007 Masters*

"MUSIC is one of mankind's greatest and oldest gifts and is a wonderful answer for peace." —*Simon Estes famed opera singer from Centerville*

VOODLAND TREASURES. A wide variety of wildflowers grows in Iowa's mbers—some used for home remedies as colorful as their petals. Add ome wild violets to salads: blossoms for color and leaves for vitamin C.

PRISTINE STREAM. The Turkey River flows through Alvin's timber on its way to the Mississippi. Trout thrive in the clear waters.

CURE FOR THE BLUES. Pioneers used bluebells for a spring tonic. Little is known whether it worked, but just the sight of those growing in Alvin's timber is sure to perk you up.

240 Mules Powered Iowa's Biggest Farm

Mammoth 6,500-acre spread near Odebolt was held in awe in early 1900s.

136 LONG EARS. We studied the top photo closely and in all counte
17 teams, which totals 68 mules one behind the other. Lower phot
shows the huge mule barn and one of the four diagonal lanes at lef

By Roy Reiman

"IT was quite a place—a real 'showplace'. It was beautiful!"

That's how Jake Ohden once described the famed Adams Ranch that loomed large at the southwest edge of Odebolt.

Ohden worked as a cook and laborer at the Adams spread, which at over 6,500 acres was the largest farm in Iowa in the early 1900s. Just a mention of the ranch still brings back a flood of memories for "seasoned" Sac County residents.

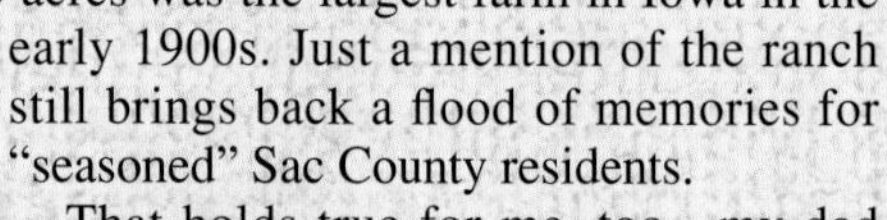

That holds true for me, too—my dad took me there once when I was around 12, and I never forgot it. The place was Ponderosa-like, much like the western ranches I later saw on TV. To discover there was an operation this incredibly immense amid the small farms around it was unfathomable.

I've wanted to share that memory with our readers for some time. So, during one of my recent trips back home, I rounded up a group of locals and asked them to share their own recollections of the place.

We gathered over coffee and cookies at the bank in Odebolt... which, by the way, was built and owned by the Adams family, providing clear evidence of a farm so big it had its own bank.

Vivid memories poured out as the group reminisced for nearly 2 hours. Most had relatives who worked on the "Adams Ranch", as it was known. One of them, Roger Rector, lived there during his early years while his father was the ranch manager.

Here are some of those recollections—jotted down as best a
I could keep up with them—but verified later before this wer
to print:

- The ranch was originally owned by Hiram Wheeler, wh bought 7,000 acres from the Iowa Railroad Land Company i 1871 for $3 an acre. In 1896, Wheeler sold it to W.P. Adams for reported $185,000. And it was Adams who turned the 6,500-ac spread into the kind of place that struck awe among neighborin farmers who were struggling to handle 240 acres.
- In all, the ranch covered 10 square miles. Crops wer planted pretty much in complete sections—corn in one sectio oats in another, hay in another, etc. Cottonwood trees lined th roadways around each section. Oats and timothy were raised fo mule feed—the 240 mules alone consumed the yield from ove 200 acres of corn.
- The ranch headquarters was located in the center sectio Four tree-lined lanes led diagonally from each corner to a larg

luster of buildings at the center—a magnificent main home, the nassive mule barn, grain storage buildings, blacksmith shop, nachine sheds, employee houses, mess hall, bunkhouses and ven its own water tower.

• At its peak, 120 teams of mules were hitched up each day. No horses were used for fieldwork; Adams insisted solely on nules.

• The scenes in the field were sometimes enough to make assersby stop on the road...to watch 40 teams of mules four breast, one behind the other, drawing harrows that covered 62 cres in a day. At corn harvest, 76 mule-drawn wagons moved n a long line, each man husking 60 bushels by hand daily for 60 onsecutive days...which resulted in up to five railroad carloads f corn shipped daily from Odebolt.

• In the early years, the ranch raised a vast amount of heep, with up to 100,000 grazing at various times. Adams then witched to cattle feeding, and did so big-time. His purchase of ,000 head of Hereford cattle in a single day at the Sioux City tockyards required three shipments by rail. At one point, 22,000 ead of cattle were eating 300 tons of silage a day.

• Up to 150 men were employed during the summer season nd 45 during the winter months. Most were immigrants from arious countries, resulting in numerous languages being spoen. Many from Italy were often heard singing Italian opera as ney worked.

• Most laborers arrived by rail at the Odebolt depot. From nere they walked to the ranch. So they didn't have to walk a nuddy path while carrying their belongings, Adams built a sidewalk from the depot to the ranch that stretched over 1-1/2 miles ong. Part of that sidewalk remains today.

• The wages weren't much—$6 a day—but the help was well-fed with "three squares a day". Newspaper clippings quote Ohden as saying: "It was amazing how much these men could at. Breakfast eggs were served eight to a platter, and some guys would pick up the platter and eat all eight. Some guys could eat even pork chops, seven roasting ears and two pieces of pie."

• For several summers, the ranch sported a semipro baseball team. "They played every Sunday afternoon," an early clipping states. "They were real bare-knucklers and would take on anybody."

• One of Adams' sons became an avid saddle and harness horse enthusiast, with his prize horses competing across the country. To accommodate them, a stable and full-scale track were built at the ranch.

• During WWII, when farm labor was hard to find, over 100 prisoners of war were sent to the ranch to work in the fields.

• One man worked full-time maintaining the cottonwood trees that outlined every section. The trees were later cut and sold to a box factory, then replaced with American elms. But in 1966, Dutch elm disease attacked the ranch, and by 1976 not one elm tree was left standing.

• The first acre of soybeans in Sac County was planted on an experimental basis on the ranch. Henry Ford reportedly encouraged Adams to plant soybeans as a commercial crop, but no large fields were ever planted during Adams' domain.

The ranch was passed from Adams to his two sons after he died. The two sons had different ideas on how the place should be run. That was evidenced when the younger son sold off all the horses and burned the carriages the day after the older son passed away.

The last of the three generations sold his holdings in 1963, and since then the property has been subdivided and has had several owners. Douglas Stenoien now owns the ranch headquarters, and a sign on the gated entrance indicates it's available for tours if prearranged.

Yes, the Adams Ranch was quite a place—a real "showplace". It was beautiful!

A TOWN IN ITSELF. The ranch covered 10 square miles. The complex of buildings at its headquarters included its own water tower and bunkhouses for 150 employees. The mess hall served "three squares a day".

The Day Things Got Out of Odor

W.P. ADAMS could sometimes be thoughtful and generous.

For example, he laid down a 1-1/2-mile-long sidewalk from Odebolt to his ranch to make the hike easier for laborers arriving by rail. And when the town decided to build a swimming pool, he donated the property and helped with the fund-raising.

But he wasn't without an ego. A case in point was chronicled in the 1977 edition of the *Odebolt Messenger*:

Adams offered to pave the streets of Odebolt if the town would change its name to Adamsville. When the city fathers turned down the request, he dumped loads of manure on the streets across town.

He claimed it was so his mules wouldn't slip on the ice when hauling grain to the elevator. But the move left both the town and Adams with a bad odor.

IO-WAYS

Featuring a springtime photo tour of our byways and backroads.

Mellow comes to mind as we think of springtime in Iowa.

After the sharpness of winter and the blustery winds f March, spring unfolds as gently as the petals of a daffodil.

Breezes are balmy and perfumed with the scent of wild plum lossoms. And unlike the scorching days of summer, the sun's ys are soothing—almost therapeutic—as they spread dappled ght on the wildflowers growing on the forest floor.

Even storms are generally mild…marked by the distant murmur of thunder, soon followed by the patter of raindrops falling on tender leaves and shoots.

And at the end of a spring day, there's stillness in the air…almost as if Nature is holding her breath in anticipation of an even more delicate day tomorrow.

Come along and join us for a photo tour—and soak in the magic of this special time of year in Iowa.

BLOOMERS in more ways than one are Dutchman's-breeches. You'll find them blooming in the timber in early spring.

Gerald Rowles

ELEGANCE. That's about the only way to describe the breathtaking beauty of a graceful great egret as it takes flight over wetlands in central Iowa.

PARK IT FOR A DAY. Watch spring unfold at Ledges State Park near Boone, or take off your shoes and go wading in the creek at left.

Marty Hulsebos

Joseph Stanski

WE'RE PUMPED ABOUT SPRING—and so are these ga den phlox putting on a show around the ol' water pum

SLEEPY MORN. There's nary a ripple at Bonnifield Lak in Jefferson County, where hints of ground fog linge over the waters. It's an easy-does-it kind of mornin

MARCHING ARCHES. Distinctive arches of the Lake City Bridge seem to bound over the North Raccoon River at Rainbow Bend in Calhoun Count

ATER OVER THE DAM—there's been a lot of it since Pine Creek Mill was built in 1848 in what's now Wildcat Den State Park near Muscatine.

Gerald Rowles

Gerald Rowles

RINGING IN THE SEASON. These Virginia bluebells do it in style with their delicate, frilly blossoms.

Gerald Rowles

CURE FOR WHAT AILS YOU. Native Americans once used columbine to treat heart trouble, headaches, kidney and bladder problems. Nowadays it just cures spring fever!

WATCH YOUR STEP—but it's difficult to do because there are so many sights to behold along this stairway in Ledges State Park in Boone County. Race you to the top!

Gerald Rowles

Gerald Rowles

Gerald Rowles

STEALING THE SHOW. It's hard to top the beauty bloodroot blooming in spring in Iowa's woodlanc

ANDY DAWN. Golden reflections from the ouds shimmer on the water as the sun rises ver Shettler Pond in Polk County...with only the ccasional hoot of an owl to break the silence of is tranquil morning. It's gonna be a great day!

'S SMOOTH SAILING for a kayaker as he ides past redbuds coloring the shore of Lake hquabi in Warren County. Ahquabi is a fitng Indian name meaning "resting place".

URN THE PAGE and you'll see spring descendg upon a winding road in the Loess Hills of estern Iowa. When we say our photograhers travel the backroads to capture glimpses f our state's scenic beauty, we're not kidding!

This photo and next page: Gerald Rowles

LIKE SNOWFLAKES. But actually, bloodroot is one of the first harbingers of spring. This pretty patch was blooming in the forest at Dickson Timber Preserve in Carroll County.

Robert Buman

NO BANKERS' HOURS HERE. A Kossuth County farmer has lots of acres to cover before quittin' time. It's a scene repeated across the state as corn planters roll this time of year.

Greg Latza

Gerald Rowles

Don Poggensee

CURIOUS KITS watch from their den as ou photographer snaps a photo. They're cute little ras cals—so long as they stay clear of the henhouse

This photo and next page: Gerald Rowles

WILIGHT TIME in Bremer County. We can't think of a bet-
er way to end a lovely spring day than to be sitting on
he island in this pond—with pant legs rolled up and bare
eet dangling in the water—just watching the sun go down.

HE BACKROADS BECKON. Wonder what beauty lies beyond
he hill on this quiet country road in Allamakee County.

URN THE PAGE and you'll see wisps of cotton-candy clouds
oating above well-kept farmsteads, adding sweetness to a
anquil spring day in the farm country of Chickasaw County.

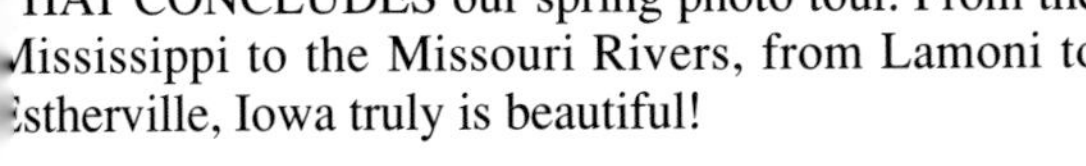

HAT CONCLUDES our spring photo tour. From the
Aississippi to the Missouri Rivers, from Lamoni to
stherville, Iowa truly is beautiful!

Yesteryear in My Hometown

Holmes is just a wide spot in the road these days. But this native son's recollections remain vivid...and just might trigger memories of the town where you grew up.

By Gene Koltvet, Mission Viejo, California

THE YEAR is 1940, the road through town is gravel, and there are no streetlights. The only lighting at night comes from the front windows and signs of the four businesses that stay open after dark—three gas stations and a country store.

There is only one business on the west side of the road, a country store operated by Ted and Helen. Two floodlights are focused down on a big yellow and green sign above the entrance that reads "Jack Spratt Foods".

A sidewalk stretches across the front of the store and the building next door. The town's hand-operated water pump stands as a sentinel at the end of the sidewalk.

On the east side of the road, at the north end, a large D-X sign lighted by floodlights on both sides stands over the canopy covering two dimly lit gas pumps—one for regular, the other for high-test gas.

Sanford, the owner, scurries around dressed in grease-stained coveralls, pumping gas, washing the windshield and checking the oil and water in an occasional customer's car.

"Each morning, a sack of mail is thrown out the railroad mail car..."

Hanging from the ceiling, a 60-watt bulb lights a dusty, pape cluttered desk. A display of engine oils occupies the corner b the window, and a peanut and gum ball vending machine stan near the door.

In the rear is an auto garage bay with a chain hoist attached the roof that's used to lift engines out of cars. A large L-shap workbench is covered with end wrenches, socket wrenche large and small ball-peen hammers, screwdrivers, grease ra and other tools of Sanford's trade.

Ring of Blacksmith's Hammer

A blacksmith shop shares an adjacent wall with the garag Two unique sounds define th work being done in this mag place:

There's the waltz-time ring o the blacksmith's hammer, thu ting ting, thunk ting ting, as bounces off the anvil...and the rhythmic thud of a mechaniz trip hammer pounding relentlessly on a red-hot plowshare.

ALL AGLOW. Like the author of the story, Osceola County Hawk-E Dianne Raveling has warm memories of the little village of Cloverda located near Sibley. "It's where I grew up and still live," she sa

Side Note: The man is happiest who lives from day to day and asks no more, garnering the simple goodness of life.

Ed, the blacksmith, stands over the anvil in his undershirt pro-
ected by a large leather apron covering him down to his knees.
t deflects sparks that fly from the red-hot iron he is shaping.

His skullcap is soaked with sweat, and even more sweat drips
rom his eyebrows and from the end of his nose. Searing heat
rom an open forge and the smell of acetylene mix together and
ermeate the air.

Next door is a sandwich shop/barbershop—a large room with
a barbershop screened off by tar-paper walls in the front corner,
and a lunch counter with six round stools in the middle of the
oom. An apartment for the owners, Bernard and Genevieve, is
artitioned off in the rear.

They operate this business together—she runs the lunch coun-
er and he is the barber.

Behind the lunch counter is a propane gas stove, small Norge
efrigerator, and a work table with a shelf above displaying
niniature boxes of Corn Flakes, Post Toasties, All-Bran, Grape-
Nuts, Puffed Wheat, doughnuts, loaves of bread and hamburger
uns.

A large dishpan sits at the far end of the counter holding dirty
lishes and glasses. Water for washing comes from the town
pump across the road and is then heated on the stove. The dishes
are washed by hand.

Pumps Gas at Post Office

The owner of the old roller-skating rink modified it to create an apartment in the rear for his family. A radio repair shop is
outfitted in the middle, and the front corner of the repair shop is
artitioned off to serve as the local post office.

There are two gas pumps out front under the canopy. On
op of the canopy is a large glass globe lit from the inside and
"Skelly Gas" painted on the outside. Jimmy, the owner, wears
a hard-billed hat that has a red and white patch on the front that
also reads Skelly. A general-purpose rag hangs out of his back
pocket.

Jimmy is also designated as the Postmaster. Townsfolk are
assigned a post office box for their mail as there is no residential
mail delivery.

Each morning as the train passes through town, a sack of mail
is thrown out of the railroad mail car. Leon, a local resident paid
to do so by the U.S. Postal Service, picks it up and delivers it to
the post office.

Each evening the day's mailbag is carried back to the train
and thrown into the mail car while it moves slowly through town.
It stops only when the bag is too big for Leon to throw.

Supplements His Pension

The last business in town is another gas station—a tiny one
at that. Art, the owner and father of four, survives on a meager
government pension as a result of being gassed on the battlefront
in France in WWI. To supplement his pension, he built a small
gas station on the corner of his residential lot.

A floodlight shines on a round orange sign, which says "Royal
400 Oil Co." The station consists of two gas pumps, a cramped
room with a desk, a couple of chairs and a rack displaying engine
oils and antifreeze.

A pit is located alongside the station, allowing an attendant to
crawl under a car to change the oil. Nearby is a large barrel filled
with kerosene for use in home lamps and lanterns.

So ends the tour of my hometown. Time keeps moving on,
leaving only memories of remembered places that no longer
exist.

Side Note: Without dreams, there is no need to work. And without work, there is no need to dream.

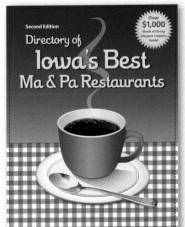

The Prettiest Farm in Iowa

WELCOME TO OUR GARDENS. A metal sign inside one of Karen's many flower beds welcomes visitors to enjoy the color of the gardens. Below: Stonypoint is the bluff where Poortingas built their new home.

Photos: Gerald Rowles

Nothing symbolizes our state like proudly primped and painted farmsteads. We showcase one of the prettiest in each issue.

WHEN Melvin and Karen Poortinga built their new Jasper County home in 1997, they came up with the perfect landscaping plan. According to Melvin, "Karen tells me what she'd like next, and I build it for her!"

Reasnor

Take one look at the unique structures and flower beds on this issue's "Prettiest Farm in Iowa" and you'll agree their plan is working to perfection!

Poortinga Farms consists of 1,300 acres of corn and soybeans near Reasnor. The home place was purchased in 1868 by Karen's great-great-grandfather, whose son began farming the land with his new bride. "Stonypoint" is

DUTCH SENTINEL STANDS WATCH OVER STONYPOINT. Melvin builds most of the unique landscaping structures over winter in his workshop, including this replica of an old Dutch windmill that turns in the wind. "It wasn't easy getting the windmill moved," Melvin chuckles.

TRIPPIN' IN THE '46 CHEVY (below left). Grandkids Tyler, 13, and Madison, 10, enjoy riding in Grandpa's truck. Melvin and Karen's daughter, Cindy, sits with husband Wayne.

A JOHN DEERE BUILT FOR TWO. Melvin and Karen Poortinga sit atop their 1963 JD 3010, with son Kevin alongside. The tractor—in its original work clothes—heads to many parades.

Side Note: In times of test, family is best.

Side Note: Coffee. Garden. Coffee. Does a good morning need anything else?

REFLECTIONS ON A SUMMER DAY. Cool off with a swim or ju take a shady walk through the covered bridge built by Melvin. Le A carved eagle keeps a close eye on the South Skunk River Valle

the name of the bluff on which Melvin and Karen's home sit The view from up there includes lush farm fields and fores land along the South Skunk River that flows through the vall below.

Thrifty Dutchman

The 3-acre home site provides plenty of elbow room f Melvin to display his landscaping handiwork—and for Karen dream up new projects.

"I guess it's the old Dutchman in me," admits Melvin, "b I like to use stuff I have lying around the farm when buildir things for our yard."

An old teardown barn provided lumber for structures like t covered bridge and waterwheel down by the pond, a gazebo ar the windmill that pays homage to their Dutch heritage.

"I built most of the structures inside my shop during t winter and then moved them outdoors when the weather coo erated," Melvin explains.

There's a guest cabin up the hill from the pond…with its ow outhouse. But don't let the rustic half-moon cut into the sic of the outhouse fool you—this privy is primo and has its ow indoor plumbing.

"After I finished the cabin, I realized it needed an outhouse Melvin chuckles.

Stonypoint also features a small barn, complete with a slee ing loft, its own kitchen and enough seating to hold about 8 people. "We mainly use it for family get-togethers and oth social gatherings," notes Karen.

Adds Melvin: "It's also a wonderful place to hold Bible

LOOMIN' FLOWERS EVERYWHERE! The 'rds are flat out of luck on washday—Karen ven fills the washtub with her pretty flowers.

KICKING BACK AT THE SHADY REST. Melvin built the guest cabin, along with most of his landscaping creations, out of lumber saved from an old barn torn down on the farm. "It doesn't have running water, but our family is welcome to spend a night here if they want," says Melvin.

HHH...THE MEMORIES. Karen surprised Melvin with a 1960 Chevy Impala, the same model he owned when they were married, for his 60th birthday.

NOT YOUR FATHER'S OUTHOUSE. The privy might look like one Dad's told you about, but this one has indoor plumbing. There's no Sears catalog inside, either!

A GOOD-SIZE MACHINE SHED. Colors of green and red paint Melvin's miniature machinery collection, displayed in a cabinet in his offic

LANDSCAPER'S DREAM. Melvin and Karen built their new home on 3 acres near their original farmstead. It's plenty roomy for many colorful flower gardens and unique creations.

PAUL BUNYAN GARDENED HERE. Karen bought this 7-foot garden trowel in Des Moines, for a donation to a homeless shelter.

FLORAL MEDLEY. The birds nesting here may need sunglasses when they peek out and see the bright colors in this garden. "My favorites are the lilies and hydrangeas," says Karen.

udies with members from our church."

And just what do you do with one of those old wire corncribs? lelvin's solution: Build a fire ring inside with benches placed ound it.

"We can sit and just enjoy the fire, or it's large enough for the mily to cook hot dogs or toast marshmallows," he says.

A Dozen Flower Beds

Colorful flowers brighten the landscaping surrounding the me. "There are probably a dozen different flower beds," Karen gures, "but when we're watering them on a hot summer day, it ems there are closer to 25!"

She says it's hard telling how many bedding plants she sets it every spring—but "it's several carloads". Melvin's sister ancy and her daughter Neva, both Master Gardeners, help with me of the plantings.

Her favorite flowers? "Probably the lilies and the hydranas," says Karen.

Life on the farm is not all flowers and work for Karen and lelvin. Family is important to them and always close by.

Their daughter, Cindy, her husband, Wayne, and their two children live across the road in the older farm home. Cindy teaches second grade at Knoxville. Wayne works at Vermeer in nearby Pella and helps out with farm work when he can.

The Poortingas' son, Kevin, lives in Indianapolis.

A metal sign in one of Karen's flower beds says, "Come into the garden…my flowers want to meet you." We're glad we did, because now all of our readers have a glimpse of one of the Prettiest Farms in Iowa.

NOTES FROM NOTEWORTHY IOWANS...

"I WAS so naive as a kid that I used to sneak behind the barn and do nothing." —*Johnny Carson*
Tonight Show host from Corning

"I LEARNED that if you have to tell somebody what you've done, it's not worth much." —*Gary Thompson*
All-American basketball player and all-around good guy from Roland

Side Note: Every path has a few puddles.

'We're Raising Hay, Cattle And Little Ranchers'

Join us as we wander with another reader down her favorite rustic roads.

AT HOME ON THE RANGE. "My husband, Scott, on his gelding 'Reno', was gathering a group of cattle to be worked with help from family friend Jimy Marten," says Iowa farm and ranch woman Kim Powell.

THE CREW. "That's me and our son Cody on my horse, Scott and son Owen in a family portrait at the headquarters of our Diamond P Ranch."

By Kim Powell, Blue Grass

WELCOME to the Diamond P Ranch, located a couple of stone throws from the Mississippi River near the small town of Blu Grass in Scott County.

The land has been in my husband Scott's family for ov 100 years, but it hadn't seen livestock in some time. Scott to over in 2004—and I came into the pictu in 2005. That's when we started the ranc

Blue Grass

But the "big bosses" of this operati are our sons Owen, 4, and Cody, 2. The were joined by a brand-new baby ranche Levi, born a month before this issue w printed. The kids are a constant joy, and we're hoping that o day they'll carry on with the ranch we're building.

Our cattle operation is currently more of a hobby than a b outfit, but our commercial herd of crossbreds is growing as w continue to keep our own replacement heifers.

We calve in early spring, and the calves are in the feedlot b October.

Cattle Handled "Cowboy Way"

Almost all of our cattle work is done on horseback with the he of a few close friends. That's not the way most Midwesterne work their cattle, but we enjoy our horses—there's just som thing about watching the cows and calves from the saddle.

We also just started to build a herd of registered Herefor with the idea of selling club calves. The Herefords are definite quieter than our crossbreds. As the boys get older and insist

"WE'RE SO BLESSED to spend our days working the land as a family. Here Scott and Owen are off to check the cows."

Side Note: Don't spur a willing horse.

OP HAND is how we refer to our good friend Jim ifert. He's been working around cattle for many year, and he truly enjoys the cowboy lifestyle."

MAKIN' HAY THE NEWFANGLED WAY. "We put up large square bales like Scott's doing here, as well as small bales. You can't quite see him, but Cody's riding with Dad."

on helping, it'll be nice knowing they can ease into it with ca that are on the gentle side.

We're also excited to see what the future holds for the k when they start showing some of those club calves. It won't too many years from now!

We farm nearly 1,000 acres and also do some custom farmi for others. Guess you might say the crop farming is to supp our ranching habit!

About 100 acres of our cropland is in hay. We sell both la and small square bales, and with the automated equipment have nowadays, haymaking sure is a lot easier than it used to That's one job we're glad we don't have to do with horses!

We're located down where the Mississippi actually flo west instead of south. The coffee is always on, and there' horse ready to go for a ride.

NOTES FROM NOTEWORTHY IOWANS...

"IT WASN'T my good looks that made me successful; it was my good planning. It wasn't my grade point; it was my guts.'

—Marvin Pomerantz, businessman from Des Moines

"I BELIEVE that in the world we have to be committec people—we are the hands and feet of God."

—Former Governor and U.S. Senator Harold Hughes from Ida Grove

NEVER TOO YOUNG TO LEARN. "Looks like Scott's having a teachable moment with Cody about hay quality as he inspects a bale of alfalfa."

SHOWING 'EM THE ROPES. "Owen and older cousin Tanner during Tanner's annual summer visit—Tanner loves being a 'ranch kid' for a few day

Side Note: If you carry your childhood with you, you never become older.